White Sky

Memoir amid Lockdown

Margrethe Alexandroni

Paperback edition first published in the United Kingdom
in 2021 by aSys Publishing

Hardback edition first published in the United Kingdom
in 2021 by aSys Publishing

eBook edition first published in the United Kingdom
in 2021 by aSys Publishing

Cover images © Adobe Stock

A CIP catalogue record for this book is available from
the British Library.

ISBN: 978-1-913438-41-8

aSys Publishing 2021
http://www.asys-publishing.co.uk

Dedicatd to
Adam and Sam

Acknowledgements

A special thank you to my sons, Adam and Sam, for introducing me to Budapest and Berlin and for making my life in lockdown bearable with calls and visits.

A big thank you to my friend and colleague, Chris Dillon, for his tireless and dedicated proofreading, for constructive comments and for pointing out minor flaws and repetitions, and for help with the Chinese proverbs. But most of all for encouraging me to carry on when I felt the project was not working and was ready to give up on it.

Also, a thank you to Janet Haney and Dr Helga Hlaðgerður Lúthersdóttir, without whose input the section on Iceland could not have been written.

Thanks also to Joanna Bergin for allowing me to use sections of her late mother's, Edith Aron's book, *The False Houses*, and for making sure that all the details are correct.

My thanks also to Nicola Mackin FRAS of aSys Publishing for her professionalism and continued support and friendship. And, for invaluable computer advice. Most of all, however, I would like to thank her for turning yet another manuscript into a book.

Book
One

雨過天晴

Rain passes; the sky clears.
Chinese proverb

March 4th, 2020

The world lies listless below a heavy layer of cloud, making the sky look grey and impenetrable. Trees are stretching their naked branches towards a sky where there is no light to be had. Outside her window people in black are hastening past, some with their hoods pulled up half covering their faces, others struggling to hold on to wind-battered umbrellas. Only one man is different, jogging along, wearing pale-blue shorts and a white T-shirt, the same colour as his hair. He reminds her of an Englishman in shorts and T-shirt she once saw in Istanbul in February – long white legs emerging from white shorts, hurrying along like a spectre amongst Turks dressed in dark coats and heavy jackets. At least she assumed he was English; he could have been any North European nationality. Leena and Tom knew it would not be warm, but they thought the same coats they wore in England would suffice. They did not, and they ended up wearing everything they had brought, one item on top of the other.

She can no longer remember how long they spent in Istanbul, but judging by all the things they did and saw, it must have been more than a long weekend. It was definitely during her February half-term. Their old world was still intact, both of them in full employment. No sign of Tom's high blood pressure and subsequent heart problems that were to claim his life eight years later. Tom had set it all up and booked them into a small hotel in the old town overlooking the Blue Mosque and the Hagia Sophia. She'll never forget the white birds circling around the floodlit Blue Mosque at night, or the massive stone walls and splendour of the Hagia Sophia. Pure magic. Or at breakfast, looking down at two of the world's most beautiful and iconic buildings with the Strait of Bosporus in the background, eating fresh pastries with quiet Turkish music playing in the background. Life doesn't get better than that.

*

Her iPhone makes a sharp vibrating noise. It is called Cosmos and she chose it because it is different from the pling-sound that usually warns of incoming text messages and e-mails. She hastens to open it in a vain hope that somebody has sent her a personal message. It does happen, sometimes several times a day, but this time, no such luck.

It is from Daily Mail News. Leena doesn't buy or read The Mail, but somehow, she got onto their mailing list, and now they are bombarding her with news around the clock. This one reads:

Breaking News: *Release of new Bond film "No Time to Die" is pushed back due to coronavirus outbreak. The 25th Bond adventure was originally scheduled to be released on March 31st, but now will not be released until November following careful consideration.*

An hour ago, there was another message: *Thirty-four new coronavirus cases are recorded in the UK as infection toll reaches 85. Coronavirus will kill Britons, warns England's Chief Medical Officer, Professor Chris Whitty. He says UK epidemic is now "highly likely" and wearing masks will not stop infections.*

Before that there was another post: *Italy closes all schools and universities to stop virus spreading. Italy's coronavirus death toll hits 107 just weeks after first case in the country—as all schools and universities and sporting venues are locked down and authorities plan a ban on KISSING.*

Something is about to grab hold and engulf them all.

March 8th, 2020

2020, a special sounding year, not simply a new decade. Such a date only comes around once every century: 1818, 1919 and now 2020. Leena is writing with a pen she bought on a whim in the Harry Potter shop in Gatwick's North Terminal. That was on February 11th, nearly a month ago. She was flying EasyJet to Berlin to visit Allan and Elida and the girls, Amelia six and a half and Lea two and three months. A happy day. True to her year-long habit, Leena was at the airport an hour before she needed to be. To pass the time she wandered into the Harry Potter shop.

Her Norwegian family laughs at her insistence to be at the airport earlier than need be. They prefer to leave home at the last minute. But what is really to be gained by sitting around chatting for an extra half hour, distracted, as in your mind you're already on your way. One summer springs to mind. The boys, Allan and Sam, must have been about nine and five. They had been spending a month in Norway with her mother. One of her nephews, Olav, then in his mid-20s, had offered to drive them to the airport, only some 45 minutes' drive away, but awkward to get to by public transport.

Olav, "When's your flight?"

Leena, "At ten past three, but remember we have to be at the airport two hours before that."

"You don't have to be there two hours in advance."

"I know, but I like to have enough time. There might be queues at the check-in."

"OK, I'll pick you up at 12:15 then."

12 noon. They are packed and ready. The boys messing about. Her mother chatting away about something from her youth as is her habit these days. Leena saw her as old, although she must have been younger than Leena is now. Feeling lonely after losing her husband, and her younger son, John, had moved out, Berit was starved of company and conversation. So different from Leena. She lives in an empty nest too, but she has little need for conversation. She has always been silent, living her life in her mind. Meaningful conversations are fine, but social chit-chat is a pain she only endures when the situation demands it. No need for Leena to say anything, Berit does the talking. The boys growing restless and fighting. Leena telling them off, looking at her watch, looking out of the window. 12:20. No sign of Olav.

12:35, finally on their way. But then Olav had to stop for petrol. Leena should have known better than to let him drive them. She knew he was phlegmatic and prone to take his time, not a busy bone in his body. Boys bickering in the back seat. On their way again, but then the traffic ground to a near halt. Accident. Traffic barely moving.

Two smashed-up cars, not too badly. Ambulance and police car, no sign of the injured. Hysterical woman being comforted by police officer. They arrived at the airport car park without a moment to spare, a quick goodbye, and off they ran, making it to the check-in at the last possible moment. Fortunately, there was only one passenger in front of them. It could have been ten people with loads of luggage. She promised herself – never again.

*

Leena's Harry Potter pen rests heavy in her hand. It is maroon, the colour of Gryffindor, Harry Potter's house at Hogwarts. She has read all the Harry Potter books and seen all the films. The idea of a magical parallel world fascinates her no end. In these dour times it is tempting to think that there might be a dimension or universe that we cannot see. Like the Fourth Dimension where nothing in our dimension exists and vice versa. Some speculative scientists believe that Jesus made use of the Fourth Dimension, which explains the way he is reputed to have walked through walls, suddenly appearing in a room. Or people being transported over vast distances in no time at all, as in Mohamed's night journey, described in the Quran, where he is said to have travelled, on a white winged mule-like beast, to the Al Aqsa Mosque in Jerusalem where he led other prophets in prayer, and subsequently ascended to the heavens.

Leena likes to believe that such things are possible, or that a different world really exists and that we can sometimes glimpse it, when we are quiet, at peace and our minds are vacant, thinking of nothing. What else could it be, the voices she sometimes hears in her childhood home in the forest – voices floating in the air, coming from everywhere and nowhere. What could it be but the goblin people chatting in their own separate world?

The gate number of the Berlin flight still has not come up. Plenty of people about, aware of the coronavirus waiting in the wings, ready to attack. Leena thinks that perhaps she shouldn't be flying at all. But Lea's nursery is closed for the rest of the week, something to do with staff training. Elida is ill with flu, Allan has an especially busy week at work and the woman who picks the girls up from school and nursery and looks after them when needed, is also ill, so of course Nanny to the rescue, happy to help. She only booked the flight the day before yesterday. A lot of people are wearing face masks, most of them Chinese. She is used to seeing Chinese and Japanese people in face masks, but this is on a different level.

And all the time Leena can't free herself from the feeling that she should not be here at all. The sight of all the face masks is unnerving. What if she catches the virus and ends up passing it on to the little ones?

March 9th, 2020. Three weeks after returning from Berlin

Breaking News: *Coronavirus cases in the UK jump to 319 as health officials confirm that 46 more people have caught the deadly infection. Man in his 70s becomes the fifth British person to die of the coronavirus as cases jump to 321.*

Italy extends lockdown across the whole country after death toll leaps by 97 in one day to 463…as travel is restricted, people are told not to go out at night.

*

Choir practice as usual. The choir, a constant in Leena's life, for the last 12 years. She did leave it for a while, but decided she missed it and returned the following season. Nobody was any the wiser why she had suddenly left in the first place. They simply assumed that she hadn't been feeling well. There was a big hoo-ha when their conductor, an opera singer called Nancy le Fort changed rehearsals from Wednesdays to Mondays, but now that too is water under the bridge. Leena didn't feel like turning up at the practice. With the way things are going, she was wondering what was the point as there might not be a concert on April 4th. Perhaps she and everyone else went out of habit and because they didn't know what else to do. At least Nancy seemed upbeat and optimistic, so perhaps the concert would go ahead, in which case they needed all the practice they could get.

Just before they started rehearsing the following text-message from Sam arrived.

Hi lovely mama. How are you today? Not trying to cause any undue panic but…it sounds like the government is expecting the virus to spread much more in the next ten days to two weeks. I wonder if you should consider steering clear of London, and if the choir should advise anyone with mild symptoms to stay away, given that some members are over 80, it could be quite dangerous for them.

He is obviously worried about Leena having just reached the horrible big 70 – a traumatic milestone she prefers to keep quiet about. The alternative is worse, but even so … For the last 2-3 years her GP's surgery, where she never sets foot, has rung her up to ask her to come for the flu jab which they advise everybody over a certain age to have. The first time she declined on grounds of not wanting to do anything specially devised for the elderly. The subsequent times she replied that she was trying to get by without immunisations, and to stay fit by means of reasonably healthy living, and by letting her immune system cope with whatever, as it has done. Perhaps now, that everybody is under the same threat, her immune system, hopefully being strengthened by doing its own work, will stand her in good stead. She'll just have to wait and see, and hopefully it will never be put to the test.

March 10th, 2020

British Airways cancels all flights to and from Italy until April 4th amid coronavirus crises. Airline says customers with tickets until Easter holiday can rebook or refund.

BA has 60 flights per day to cities including Milan, Rome, Venice, Turin. This comes as the government said anyone travelling to the UK from Italy must self-isolate.

Health Minister Nadine Dorries tests positive for coronavirus after a week of meeting people in Parliament and attending a meeting with Boris Johnson, as UK cases rise by 61 in a day to 382.

Six people in Britain have now died from the disease with 382 infected.

March 11th, 2020

UK's seventh coronavirus patient dies: Boris Johnson is accused of playing roulette with people's lives and is urged to close schools, ban football matches and order country to work from home as WHO declares pandemic.

Italy announces all shops except pharmacies and food outlets will be closed as coronavirus death toll climbs by 31% to 827 in 24 hours, and country's top doctors should stop treating the elderly and focus on those with better survival chances.

March 12th, 2020, 10:50am

Outside the sky is blue. Only a few white clouds floating about. The naked branches of the magnolia tree outside her window is covered in bright pink buds ready to burst into bloom.

Her worries for her kind-hearted sons and beautiful little granddaughters are like a dull ache that won't shift no matter how much she struggles to ignore it. Sam lives in Walthamstow. She has begged him to stay away from the Tube during rush hour. He is 39 now, and 39-year-olds have never been known to heed their mother's advice. Usually they know better. Last night he rang Leena urging her to buy more non-perishable food. She has quite a lot in her freezer and cupboards, but far from enough for a major siege. Having passed the big 7-0 she has reached an age where she might not be treated should she get ill, or hit by a car. A frightening prospect.

And Allan is in Germany in the centre of what used to be East Berlin. Oh, how she loved to visit them ... Amelia now six and a half. Leena held her for a long time the day after she was born. She was weak and the nurses struggled to get a few drops of milk inside her. Her tiny hands felt like soft seaweed bobbing on a faint current. She had quite a lot of light-brown hair. New-borns are supposed to grip your finger if you put it inside their hand, but Amelia did not, only the faint brush of floating seaweed. Forever a pessimist seeing doom and gloom where others are hopeful and optimistic, Leena thought to herself: So, are you only going to be with us for one day then? Of course, she was not, and soon was growing in strength. But the bond between them had been forged. Fortunately, her mother had no such thoughts. Elida is a solid and practical person who takes things in her stride. Leena has never told her and Allan, but her worries for her family are always with her. Always there like the deepest string of a cello reverberating at the bottom of her heart. She doesn't worry much about herself, only about her family, anxious that something might happen to them.

Their younger daughter, Lea, was born on the Cayman Islands, and she was nearly five months old before Leena set eyes on her. She did not expect to have a close relationship with Lea at all, but she was wrong. When the family visited her two months ago, at New Year, she and Leena were singing together. Lea has a sweet little voice and holds her tune well even though she is just over two.

They were singing nursery rhymes and she looked a Leena with pure love in her eyes. What more could she ask for?

*

In Italy coronavirus cases topped 12,000 with more than 800 deaths and Europe went over the 22,000 mark.

US bans travel from Europe. President Trump suspends all travel to the US from Europe, except the UK due to coronavirus.

Tom Hanks and his wife are diagnosed with coronavirus in Australia. The 63-year-old actor announces they have caught the virus while filming in Australia and describes how it gave them symptoms like chills and body aches. Hanks and his wife, Rita Wilson, visited Australian hotspots including Sydney Opera House. Queensland premier said that anyone in contact with them would have to self-isolate.

*

UK's coronavirus death toll jumps to 10 as number of cases of the killer infection soars to 590 in Britain's biggest increase yet. Officials reveal that both patients who died had underlying conditions. One was in Essex and one was in London.

March 14th, 2020

It is reassuring to know that our friends in Europe have politicians who have their best interests at heart. Meanwhile back in the UK we're stuck with a "take it on the chin" from the part-time PM.

"Today the watchword for Europe is <u>solidarity</u>. No one will be left alone and no one will act alone." David Sassoli, European Parliament President. *"Not since the end of the Second World War, have we faced such a dramatic crisis."* *David Sassoli promising Parliament would work on the Covid-19 relief package presented by the European Commission. It consists of:*

Support for the health systems of EU countries.

Support for jobs, businesses and the economy.

In addition, at least €37 billion is ready and available from the EU budget.

It is sad to think that if we had not left the EU, some of this package would have come to us as well. And what is our beloved PM doing? Telling people over 70 to self-isolate, ostensibly for their protection, forgetting that if the virus doesn't get them, isolation and lack of exercise might. Apart from that he appears to be doing very little, except listen to a scientist's advice that once 60% of the population has been infected, herd immunity will take effect and Covid-19 will fizzle out by itself. But how many people will have died in the meantime?

Just now, Breaking News

Hancock confirms elderly WILL soon be told to stay at home for four months to stem the spread of coronavirus. This argument has one big flaw. The elderly is the group spending the most time at home anyway, and therefore the group least likely to spread the virus.

Government effectively on war footing as it tries to combat coronavirus spread.

Whole families will soon be told to stay at home if one member has symptoms.

Government urges manufacturers to make as many ventilators as possible.

Mr Hancock says NHS has 5,000 of the machines, but needs many times more.

Ministers are also buying up beds in private hospitals to boost NHS capacity.

Army could be called in to guard hospitals and supermarkets amid panic buyers.

March 15th. Outing to central London

The prospect of staying around the house, or rather within walking distance, for four months is inconceivable. And so is the thought of living through months of not being allowed to see Sam, who lives in Walthamstow on the opposite side of London. And every bit as bad, there will be no trips to Berlin for God knows how long…Leena just can't take it in, it's too heart-breaking.

So, to get out and about while she still could, she decided to venture up to London. Was it wise? Possibly not. Would she get infected? There was a chance, so of course, she was worried.

It was a Sunday, less traffic, or so she thought. She had decided to knit herself a jumper. It would give her something to do during the long evenings in front of the TV. The last time she was in the haberdashery department at John Lewis in Oxford Street, she had bought three balls of super-soft yarn in shades of blue and turquoise. The original idea was to knit a scarf. Last night, when suddenly faced with four months of isolation, she decided to buy more of the same yarn and knit a jumper instead. She also needed to get more moisturiser for her face and a couple of hair-dying kits. Already she had decided to keep up her morale by not letting herself go. Better to stock up while she had the chance.

The 20 minutes' train ride to London shouldn't be too bad, on a mid-Sunday morning and with a deadly virus keeping people from crowded spaces, trains and busses should be fairly empty, or so she thought. But alas...

The train was already quite full when she got on, seven stations from Victoria. The air felt stuffy and recycled. She looked around the carriage. All windows closed except one. She opened the one next to her. Nobody noticed or thought to follow suit. One would have thought they'd want to get in as much fresh air as possible to minimise any virus floating about, but people seemed blissfully oblivious. She could barely feel a faint draft coming in through her window. More people entered at every station. Few people left. At every stop the open doors let in some fresh air, but not enough to make a difference. Leena regretted her escapade and was seriously worried about what might be lurking in the recycled air. And people...entering, looking happy. She noticed a beautiful dark-haired young woman in a classic beige coat, happy, big smile on her face, greeting some friends already on the train. And all around, people, most of them young, but not all, chatting and talking, out for the day, not a care in the world, or so it seemed. That was when she heard her mother's voice in her ear, quiet, almost whispering: "Relax, you'll be all right, but don't do this again; the virus is all around."

At Victoria she got on the 390 bus. Normally it would leave less than half-full, but today it stood and stood until most seats were taken. Up Grosvenor Rd to Lancaster Gate. Streets chocka-block, traffic barely moving. More people entering at every stop, few getting off. A fat lady in a cobalt-blue coat plonked herself next to Leena. Too close for comfort. Leena didn't want her there, but what could she say? A family group standing by the door – a woman of at least 70 and two middle-aged men, most likely her sons. The woman looked smart in a pale-blue coat and black high-heeled shoes. They laughed and talked, unworried about being squashed up between total strangers. At Park Lane the road suddenly cleared and the bus gathered speed. Certainly a relief, but Leena couldn't forget her mother's words, "the virus is all around." Normally she would sit on the bus until Oxford Circus, but at Marble Arch she could take no more, got out and walked the rest of the way.

There was a fair amount of people in John Lewis, but you couldn't say it was crowded. Leena quickly bought the things she had come for and headed for home. Oxford Street was closed for traffic towards Marble Arch, so no bus. No alternative but to walk to Oxford Circus and catch the Victoria Line to Victoria. Normally a frequent line, but this time the display said: "next train, five minutes". The following train, however, was due only one minute after that. And all the time the platform kept filling up, mainly close to the entrance. Something she has never understood – people crowding on one part of the platform, leaving the rest nearly empty. Leena walked to the back end of the platform where there was plenty of space. She decided that if the train was totally crowded, she would wait for the next one a minute later. When the train finally arrived, it was as Leena had expected, so full that people were pressed against the doors, but still people in the crowded end of the platform were pushing to get on. At the back of the train, where Leena was waiting, there were still a few free seats, so she got on rather than waiting for the next one. Here too, people seemed unconcerned, going about their business. Three young women sitting opposite her were chatting. All three around 20, long blond hair, dark clothes. One of them was obviously telling an amusing story, because she did most of the talking whilst her friends listened and laughed. Looking at the people around her, you wouldn't think anything was amiss with the world at all.

On the train from Victoria, Leena looked up Facebook on her phone. There was a long entry from a former colleague who now lives in Vienna, and has been delighting her friends with photos of beautiful buildings and landscapes. Today was no exception. However, her entry reflected Leena's thoughts precisely: *"...Seeing friends in the UK and Iceland out and about, carrying on as normal, seems weird from over here on the mainland. We're not going to be able to leave the house for any non-urgent reason from Tuesday onwards. All social contact is forbidden. Gatherings of more than five people are banned, even in your own home. The measures will be enforced by the police and army.*

I shall miss our walks, but at least we're lucky enough to have a balcony. Am thinking about the poor souls who are going into isolation alone, especially those who are elderly and infirm. Thank God for social media which means we can all stay connected in a way we never could before. Today's walk in Lainzer Tiergarten felt all the more wonderful for being the last until God knows when."

*

And in Italy coronavirus deaths have risen by 300 overnight to bringing the total up to 1,809.

24,747 people are now infected as a terrifying video shows how a city newspaper obituary page has expanded from one to ten pages.

March 16th, 2020. There is always one.

Monday afternoon. Leena has ventured into her local M&S food store to stock up on some goodies before entering house arrest for her own protection. Although, she has no intention of staying locked in her house for four months. Who is to know if she takes a lone walk on the common after dark, and what possible harm can it do? She pities people who are too infirm to go out, and the poor souls who blindly follow rules whether they make sense or not. Luckily, she was born with a mind of her own. It would have made more sense if the government had given directives to curtail the movements of younger people, i.e. to close down public spaces like pubs, cinemas, cafés and what have you. Instead, the powers that be make do with locking up the elderly, and for the rest of the population some lame advice about keeping away from public spaces. A huge mistake, as it turned out. It was on people's minds, certainly, but on the whole people did not yet realise that if Britain had gone to lockdown on the 16th, instead of waiting for another week, thousands of lives would have been spared. Many individuals, like choir masters and people running clubs and social events had already taken matters into their own hands, used common sense, and closed up shop until further notice.

Back to Monday afternoon.

M&S is crowded. People of all ages, including many of 70+ who, according to the guidelines, should not be there, but might have hoped for a quick in and out, as did Leena when she entered. Still, things were going well. She quickly found what she was looking for – things that are difficult to buy online. She likes to look at the sell-by date to make sure it is as far into the future as possible. It's important that things like avocados and bananas are not yet ripe … She hardly eats meat, apart from a bit of smoked, crispy bacon once in a while, but it has to be extremely lean. She can't stand fat and always cuts it away.

All of this is especially important these days as this might be her last shopping expedition for the foreseeable future.

Ten minutes, and she had all that she'd come for plus two extra pizzas, to go in the freezer, and a bottle of wine. The queues at the till were not too bad. Leena joined the one that looked the most promising, as she wanted to spend as little time as possible in close proximity with others. Only two people in front of her, neither of whom had a lot of shopping. All well and good. At the moment a short white-haired lady in a grey mac, clearly past 70, was being served. Between her and Leena, a likeable-looking woman in her 50s. Behind her a man of similar age to Leena. The mood in the queue felt somewhat tense, as though nobody really wanted to be there. Leena became aware of an argument going on between the white-haired woman and the cashier, loud enough for her to hear most of it. Somehow or other the woman was entitled to a free bottle of wine. The cashier said no, it was too late. She should have thought about it before. The white-haired woman insisted. There was stale-mate. The queue behind Leena was growing longer. The argument went on. The woman in front of Leena looked at her and rolled her eyes. Leena wanted to pay up and get out. They all did. Without planning to Leena found herself calling out: "So go and get your bottle then!"

The woman, smiling: "Is that all right?" And off she went. Given the situation anyone with the tiniest bit of sense, would have been as quick as possible – right colour, right price, fine, that's my bottle. But not this woman, she was taking her time, it had to be the right wine. At long last she returned, bottle in hand. But then there was another problem, nobody quite grasped what. Possibly she wanted to get cash out after having paid her bill, when it was too late. Whatever it was, she kept insisting. The cashier looked close to a nervous breakdown. The woman in front of Leena said that in her place she would have been so embarrassed that she would have left as fast as she could. At last, with a light-hearted sorry in the direction of the people waiting, like when you accidentally bump into someone, the woman was ready to leave. Not getting the sympathetic that's-all-rights she clearly expected, she started apologising more profusely, further holding up the queue. Leena nearly shouted: "Get on with it! Just go!" And finally, she did. Leena could only hope that nobody around her was infected.

It is true that people's finances can be strained, especially for people trying to get by on a meagre pension. Still, there is a time and a place. If a free bottle of wine was such a momentous event in the woman's life, how come she only remembered it when it was too late? And knowing that people were waiting, why did she take ages choosing her bottle? But she was old, some will say, not thinking that making excuses for someone's antisocial behaviour because of their age is in itself ageist, as if expecting older people to be confused and past it.

*

Their concert had been cancelled, a unanimous decision reached by the conductor Nancy le Fort and the committee, of which Leena was a member. Consequently, nobody quite understood why Nancy still insisted on holding one last rehearsal. They were supposed to have performed Beethoven's exquisitely beautiful *Mass in C Major*, long and in places difficult. They had been practicing since the beginning of January and were finally getting it right. Everybody thought it was a shame to let it go. But what was the point of further rehearsing a piece they would not be performing?

Leena had texted Jen, who gives her a lift to practice, and Nancy, explaining why she would not be attending the rehearsal. There were vulnerable people in the choir. She had taken chances with her foray into central London by train, bus and Tube, all of them crowded, and by spending ages in a queue at M&S. There was a trip to Sainsbury's too, but more about that later. Her mother's "you'll be all right" was ringing in her ears, but that was before she had visited two crowded supermarkets. She did not wish to risk infecting the more vulnerable members of the choir.

The following day she received messages from both Nancy and Jen. Nancy wrote: "*Sorry we missed you Monday, as it was quite a special evening. Stephen brought Prosecco and Jen brought chocolates and we sang through all of the Beethoven we had done so far.*" Perhaps Nancy, a near-famous international soprano, cares more deeply about the choir than she likes to admit. Jen too told her about the Prosecco and chocolates, that only half the choir had attended, and that those who did were very happy to see each other. Leena was truly sorry to have missed it, especially with the prospect of months of isolation. It would have been her last opportunity for socialising. The thought of being cut off from her sons and granddaughters for however long it would take, brought tears to her eyes. She knew, however, that she had done the right thing.

*

Oh yes, her Sainsbury expedition ... Yesterday she also paid a visit to Sainsbury's before shunning all spaces where she'd be in close contact with others. She did buy a few things, like a loaf of raisin and walnut bread. She would have preferred an ordinary brown loaf, but this was all that was left. Even the hot crossed buns had disappeared. No eggs, she had eight at home, which would have to do. No toilet paper, no lots of things. In fact, most of the shelves were empty, cleaned out, not a sausage. People had been grabbing whatever they could lay their hands on. During a visit to Sainsbury's two days previously, she had noticed a woman with a large trolly full of toilet paper and kitchen rolls. Now certain items have been rationed to two per customer. She got two packs of minestrone cup-a-soup, a bottle of rapeseed oil, two Lintbars – dark chocolate with crushed hazelnuts. Finally, a small bottle of runny honey and a tube of Colgate to add to the two she already had. Good job she had taken Sam's advice slowly to collect things before the full onslaught of panic buying.

Breaking News

Baby tests positive for coronavirus at Norfolk hospital and is put into isolation with two other patients.

Frightening when she thinks of her two beautiful granddaughters in Berlin. It really does not bear thinking about – the lovely little girls … Until now the fact that children seemed to have been spared had somewhat put her mind at rest.

When, after a few days, Leena still had not experienced the tell-tale symptoms of headache, temperature and a cough, she knew that she'd had a lucky escape.

*

Suddenly Leena is struck by a distant memory. Seemingly out of nowhere. Oslo early 1970s. The final year of her French degree course. It had been a beautiful sunny day, one of these days when you notice; yes, spring is beginning to take hold. During the day the ice on the puddles in the walkway through the university campus had melted, but now they were covered by a thin layer of ice that crunched and cracked under their feet as they made their way from the lecture. Leena heading for her modest student room and a French-inspired meal of canned tuna, baguette and camembert. Grapes for dessert. A clear blue evening, the sun has just set behind the tall buildings of the campus, the air so thin and crisp you can taste it on your tongue. It had been a wonderful lecture, a one-off given by a postgraduate student not much older than Leena. He had talked about Albert Camus, and a short-story he had written when he was about the same age as them, but so perceptive and mature, as though written by somebody much older, yet with the acute sensuality of youth. The heat of the Algerian summer, eating a ripe peach, the juice running down his chin...A world out there that Leena dearly wanted to inhabit, and one day she would, she was sure of that, this was just a stage in-between.

The memory is so crisp and clear, as though she is still there, walking on the crunchy ice, and perhaps deep down she has been there all along, for the last 48-odd years. Perhaps the sheer awfulness of the present made it crop up in her mind. She has a feeling she was not alone, but whoever she was walking with is buried too deep in her brain to be recalled.

Medics

An anguished cry from the NHS front line: coronavirus is about to explode among medical staff. They are alarmed by the failure of the Government to take more drastic action to fight Covid-19. They are stunned that it seems to have opted for capitulation when best practice leaders in East Asia – and I don't mean China – have managed to contain the virus through use of technology, and to do so without massive economic and social disruption.

British key medical staff complain about hugely inadequate protective clothing and equipment. Front line staff such as doctors and nurses run big risks of being infected. At the same time, they are furious that they are not being tested to see if they have contracted the disease.

Hospital staff caring for the growing number of those seriously ill with the disease, fear that they could pass it on to other patients after catching it at work due to poor protection. Doctors who are dealing most closely with Covid-19 patients—A&E medics, anaesthetists and specialists in acute medicine and intensive care are most worried. A doctor in an infectious disease ward of a major UK hospital, who is treating patients with Covid-19 said: "I'm terrified. I am seriously considering how I can keep working as a doctor."

*

There was a time, a happier time, a time set to go on forever. But now, let's face it. Plans for the summer are down the drain. Life as we know it finished overnight. Not long ago we made plans assuming that tomorrow would be much like today, that this year's March would be much like last year's. Time dripping away imperceptibly, hardly noticed, just taken for granted.

March 23rd, 2020

Spring is on its way. The pink flowers on the magnolia tree Allan once gave her for Mother's Day look beautiful against the blue sky. No leaves as yet. It was only a dry stick when he brought it home, but look at it now! It nearly reaches the first-floor windows. The cobalt blue pansies she bought not long ago are doing well in their pots. She planted some yellow ones too, but the blue ones are more striking.

Leena has been living in this house, in what she thought of as an uninteresting suburb, for nearly thirty years. There were two aborted attempts to settle in her family home in Norway, but that's history. The first time an excessive snowfall and isolation forced her to leave. It was fine for a week, but one morning she woke up feeling that something was different. At first, she couldn't put het finger on it, then it dawned on her; it was the silence. She had grown up with the sound of cars driving by, some 100 metres from the house. Over the years the traffic increased and the noise turned into a hum you got so used to that you didn't really notice it until suddenly it wasn't there. She looked out of the window and all she could see was a wall of falling snow.

Five days outside time and place, sitting alone in the house, watching the snow fall. *The Sound of Silence*, a hit by Simon and Garfunkel that she loved in her youth and still does, was playing in her head. She found it on u-Tube and listened to it again and again. One of the blessings of our time is that the music of our youth, any music in fact, is available at the click of a button. Other times she would switch on the TV or search for classical music on the radio. The isolation was doing something to her mind. Her real life, the London house, her sons and granddaughters grew distant and irrelevant. Craving silence and your own company is one thing, being cut off from your life is something else. The drive to her house was blocked by waist-high snow drifts, so no chance to go food-shopping or drop in at the local café for a coffee and a cinnamon bun. Regrets from the past kept cropping up in her mind – things she'd said that shouldn't have been said, people she'd hurt without meaning to, situations she could have handled better … Allan and Sam rang her every day, but she couldn't think of anything to say to them. When a man with a snow blower finally appeared, she knew it was time to leave.

The second time was in summer. Calm and peaceful at first, but then assorted family members came trickling in – people she had little in common with except for increasingly diluted blood-ties. Not all at the same time, but there was nearly always somebody there, when Leena wanted time to herself. They had the right to stay there. The house was jointly owned by the whole family to be used as a holiday home, all of them mucking in together, cooking, relaxing, playing board games, watching TV, children running around … Leena nearly used the expression *screaming children*, but that would be unkind. All well and good, but it was not what Leena was looking for and she felt out of place and hassled. She'd had more affinity with her brother, John, but he had passed away the previous year. He was survived by his wife, Nina, who is growing more eccentric by the day, turning night into day and day into night, with her dog, Timo, running her life. Timo is a large 13-year-old chow-chow, calm and docile, a magnificent beast in his younger days, but now taking on the moth-eaten look of old age, not much in the way of a personality, or so Leena always thought. He flatly refuses to go upstairs. Perhaps he is waiting for John to come home and worrying that he might arrive when he is upstairs so he'll miss him. He was always John's dog rather than Nina's. When she goes upstairs, he stands at the bottom of the staircase howling until she comes back down. As a result, Nina has been sleeping on the living room coach ever since John passed away. The house used to look lovely, but now her collection of vases and colourful glass objects is jostling for space amid old magazines and empty coffee-cups. She lost her job in the bank due to automation a year before losing John, so here she is, unemployed and alone without the structure to her days that she clearly needs.

For years Leena felt close to her two nephews, twins Olav and Willum, nine years her juniors, sons of her older brother, Hans, who vanished without trace at the age of 22. She used to look after them when they were children. But now ... having lived in different countries with different lifestyles for so long, there is little common ground except for childhood memories. Both nephews have beautiful cars and houses. Their sons and daughters are in solid mainstream professions. Perhaps Leena is an intellectual snob, but she would dearly have loved it to be something more – eccentricities, telling her about an interesting book they have read ... something other than everyday practicalities and the here and now. But there is nothing of the kind, just houses and golf and dinner parties and skiing holidays in Austria. Fine, if that's what you want, but it just isn't Leena's world. Little evidence of what the Germans call Hinterland – background country, as in a soulless tourist ghetto that could be anywhere. If you want more from your holiday than sun bathing, eating and drinking, you've come to the wrong place.

What you see is what you get. Try to peak beneath the surface and you find very little ... people who head for pubs the minute the land in England and spend their holidays on the Costa del Sol without ever setting foot in the Alhambra.

They mean well, Leena has to keep telling herself that it is she who is different. She wanted to stay in her forest home to reflect, to figure out how best to spend whatever time is left to her, or just to be.

Many years ago, in Berlin, long before Allan and family moved there, she had spent a few days there with Tom and Sam. One evening they had gone to a pizza restaurant that Sam knew about – one of these places where you share a table with other guests, which was fine. In came three women in their 20s, and with them, a woman of advanced years. Leena assumed her to be the mother or grandmother of one them. They got talking. It transpired that the four of them were staying in a youth hostel around the corner, which was where they had just met and decided to go for a pizza together. So, there she was, a woman of 70, backpacking and striking up friendships with people decades younger. Perhaps Leena could do something like that?

One evening, she'd had a wonderful day in the forest, picking wild blueberries and strawberries – a bit late for strawberries, but plenty of blueberries. A hare, wearing its brown summer coat, had jumped out from the bushes. For a few moments it had stood watching her before hastening off like the rabbit in *Alice in Wonderland*. The voices of the goblin people had been all around, as though carried on the breeze. Impossible to make out the words, but they were there. The sun was as high in the sky as it gets up north in late August. Suddenly she became aware of her mother walking next to her, transparent at first, then more solid. She was wearing the yellow cardigan she often wore when Leena was a child. She loved walking around the forest picking berries, from the first wild strawberries in June to the last cowberries in October. You don't boil wild strawberries and cowberries, you crunch them, mix in sugar and keep stirring until the sugar is dissolved. You can't get better jam than that. Her mother was gone as quickly as she appeared, but then Leena spotted her further along, waving at her daughter to come and join her. Leena walked over and found a patch of particularly juicy blueberries. So, this was the life Berit had imagined – the two of them together, out in the forest, picking wild berries. Returning home, making jam … Perhaps, when all was said and done, not such a bad life at all. When she looks up, her mother is gone, but the long forest grass is moving imperceptibly where she stood.

She was looking forward to making fresh jam and eating it with a loaf of bread fresh from the oven. Exactly like the suppers they used to have in summer when she was a girl, like visiting her childhood. At 8pm there was a film on TV she wanted to watch. She had seen it before, an old film with Jodie Foster playing a girl who had grown up in isolation deep in the forest, with only her reclusive mother for company. She and her mother had even developed their own language. But then the mother died, and the girl, in her late teens or early 20s was discovered. A sweet film that had remained with Leena for years, and she was looking forward to see it again. She was just going to sit down and enjoy her meal, when a car drew up in front of the house. It was Willum and his wife, Kari. All smiles and-how-are-you? "We couldn't help thinking of you sitting here all on your own, so we bought pizzas and thought we'd come and keep you company." What could she say? For a moment she worried that she might miss her film, but then she decided to stand her ground. Fortunately, Kari liked the idea of their watching a film together, and it was her kind of film – no sex, bad language or violence. Willum had brought a paper, so it was all right really, but still Leena felt thwarted, and she didn't enjoy the film as much as she had expected. As they were leaving, Kari said, "We should have brought something more interesting than pizza, but at least it was better than sitting by yourself eating bread and jam."

*

On the 4th of March Leena had the idea of chronicling the advance and hopefully the demise of the coronavirus. But enough is enough. She can't take any more. Every day brings reports of increases in the death toll and it is set to continue – bodies piling up – too horrible for words. She saw a report on TV, a large London hospital ward filled with people on ventilators, fighting for their lives, doctors and nurses in space suits, face masks and visors. They said that wearing the protective gear is so hot and uncomfortable that they can only stand it for a couple of hours at the time. Still, they are the lucky ones, in other hospitals medical staff has to make do with little more than flimsy face masks and plastic aprons. A lot of people refuse to take social distancing seriously. The virus only lives in the body for 14 days, hence the 14 days quarantine for people who have been exposed to it. If during that time it has not found a new body to enter, it will die. Consequently, a policy of social distancing for however long it takes, will do the trick. Sadly, a lot of people's attitude appears to be: I'm all right, so therefore everyone I meet must be all right too. Besides, most of the people who die from the virus are old with underlying conditions.

Again and again we see this attitude reflected in the press, the implicit sentiment being that those with underlying health conditions would soon be dead anyway, so what does it matter if Covid-19 takes them now? But that's the thing, the death that doesn't matter could be anyone – your workmate, your neighbour – people who have merrily been going about their business for years, people you pass in the street showing no sign of living with an on-going condition, useful members of society, loved by family and friends, and suddenly they are made to feel that their lives don't matter. Ever since the first report of a coronavirus fatality in England, the government has been at pains to calm nerves by stressing the victim's poor health. The chief medical officer, Chris Whitty, when announcing one of the first corona-deaths uttered the following sentence: "The patient, who was being treated at the Royal Berkshire Hospital, was an older patient who had underlying health conditions." The language used by officials describing the spiralling scenarios risk dehumanising the elderly and the frail by making them feel that they don't matter. For example: Dr Nick Phin, deputy director of the National Infection Service at Public Health England, went on Newsnight and didn't blink as he nonchalantly talked about those with "pre-existing conditions" who will suffer "more serious illness and unfortunately death…" basically announcing their death sentence. How unbelievably cruel! The people concerned must surely have been listening.

But who are those people with underlying conditions whose lives don't matter? Leena can think of a few. There is Linda, 65-years-old, who has asthma, and therefore placed in the 'at risk' category. She is half Finnish and recently emigrated to Finland where she is very happy, enjoying fresh air and open countryside. She definitely wants to live and has a son who loves her. There is Antonia, Allan's mother-in-law, a vibrant woman, also 65. She had a serious heart attack four years ago, but has made a good recovery. Looking at her you wouldn't think anything was amiss. She is helping out with her grandchildren, doing her pottery, she is a ceramic artist, living a full and active life as long as she takes her medication. There is Leena's friend, Anita, a 52-year-old astronomer, who has psoriasis and has been taking immune depressants. She and her partner will spend hours outside on a freezing night to get a special shot of stellar a constellation or a satellite crawling across the moon. And of course – everybody over 70, many of whom have some health issue or other, but far from all, like her friend, Gail, 73, and her husband of similar age. Through a set of extraordinary circumstances, they have been the legal guardians and carers of a great grandchild since he was three and he is now seven. Unusual, but life doesn't always follow the rule book. Don't tell that little boy that his cherished great-grandparents are worthless people whose lives don't matter.

There was a time when Leena and Gail used to see a lot of each other. They were neighbours in North London, had the same sort of house in a cul-de-sac that had once been an apple orchard belonging to a manor house, now a shelter for the homeless. A few of the apple trees were still going strong, and their fruit was shared between the residents every autumn. Gail and her husband, Stephen, had two children, Dave and Emily, six and five years older than Allan, and much older than Sam who was only one when they moved in. Dave and Emily soon took to Allan and Sam. It was Dave who got Allan into watching Star Wars films, and he has been a fan ever since. Emily loved looking after little Sam. So, naturally enough, Gail and Leena became friends. Gail was teaching French in a rough comprehensive, and Leena was scratching an income from freelance teaching, translating, and writing short stories for Scandinavian magazines. The two husbands had less of an affinity and didn't see much of each other. It was a happy time. Gail and Leena in and out of each other's homes, taking their children on outings. Leena remembers that Gail drove them all the way to Selfridges to see Father Christmas. In summer they would go to a local open-air swimming pool … things like that.

The family lived in the orchard for seven years and four months. It was their home. But then Tom was offered a position on the opposite side of London that only an idiot would have turned down. Leena's heart was bleeding as they packed up their belongings. She didn't want to leave, and neither did the boys. One of the things she enjoyed was to look out of her kitchen window on a Saturday morning and see groups of Jewish people, all dressed up, on their way to synagogue, an exotic sight you'd never see in Norway where you seldom saw anyone who was not an ethnic Norwegian. She had several Jewish friends. One of them was Judy from Berlin, a vibrant woman that Leena is proud to call her friend. Her mother was a doctor who had survived the war without leaving Berlin by going underground, quite literally, hiding in the basement of the hospital where she had used to work. Leena and Judy are still in touch.

Over the years Leena and Gail saw increasingly less of each other, but when they did, it always felt as though they had seen each other only last week even though a couple of years might have slipped by. The last time they met up was during what Leena has come to see as the last days, only she was not aware of it at the time. Now she can see that they were already balancing on the edge of an abyss. She had often thought along those lines in relation to climate change, but never had she imagined that the fall into the abyss would be that imminent.

A meet-up had long been planned, and finally they had got it together. Leena is looking at the entry in her 2020 diary, one of the last: *January 24, Friday. Meet Gail,*

British Museum. A couple more entries, and the diary is blank—a year of nothing. They had agreed to meet up for a coffee in one of the two cafeterias on the ground floor. It was the day Sam had gone to Sarajevo to do research for a book about people in conflict zones that he was thinking of writing. There is a photo of Sam standing in the snow-clad hills above Sarajevo, dated January 27, the hood of his coat pulled up over his woolly hat, big smile on his face. Later he told Leena about the siege of Sarajevo when civilians were trapped inside the city and only those with money to buy a pass were allowed to leave. 13,000 Bosnian Serbs were encircling the city. Their snipers taking position in the surrounding hills and mountains. From there residents were relentlessly and indiscriminately bombarded by mortar shells and suffered under constant fire from snipers. There was hardly any food, and no electricity, no heat and no water. People risked their lives queuing for hours to collect water from fountains in full view of the snipers who had fun choosing their victims. The war ended in December 1995, and on February 29th 1996 the Bosnian government declared the siege over. By the end of the siege 13,352 people had died, including 5,434 civilians—and a beautiful old city was in ruins. Strange how a conflict can escalate and make people who have been living contentedly together for generations suddenly hate each other. Leena never fully understood what the conflict was actually about, perhaps nobody really knew ... and what it was that suddenly made ordinary people like electricians and post office workers commit acts of terrible cruelty. There is another photo taken on the 26th. It's nearly dark. Sam is standing in the middle of a square, in front of what looks like a Byzantine church – in the light from the street lamps you can see the falling snow. His arms are held high, as if shouting "Yes!" overcome by the beauty of the scene. Somehow, this photo gave Leena the idea of visiting Transylvania later in the year to see the landscapes of Bram Stoker's Dracula. She would love to write a gothic novel one day, if only she had the talent – so perhaps something less ambitious like a short story. She might still make it, and Sam might get to explore another conflict zone. Time will tell.

Suffice to say that Leena and Gail spent four wonderful hours together, first at the museum and then at a neighbouring Turkish restaurant called Taz, where they had mezzes. A restaurant that funnily enough they were both familiar with, totally independent of each other. Leena had been there several times with colleagues from her university department, and Gail had been there with friends. Stephen was picking up their great grandson from school and everything was as good as could be.

*

For the last few days, Leena has written nothing at all, nor has she been reading the ever-depressing *Breaking News*. She is leading a solitary existence in her home interspersed with one single walk a day, work in the garden and chats with neighbours, at a safe distance, when she happens upon them in the street. No social activity planned, or anything else, like a visit to the cinema. Hankering back to better times, Herne Hill Station keeps cropping up in her mind, conjuring up memories of when there was a life out there, and she was part of it. Memories overshadowing the grim realities of the present.

Herne Hill is a small station on the line to London Victoria. Insignificant and unexciting, yes, but the Thames Link service stops there. North-bound to Elephant & Castle, Black Friars, Farringdon, St Albans, Luton Airport and Bedford. The south-bound trains stop at a number of stations in the south-west London suburbs. A station she had passed thousands of times on her way to and from work, giving it no thought at all.

But then Sam moved to Budapest with his Hungarian girlfriend Aurora, and the most economical way of getting there was by Wizz Air from Luton.

More than three years now since she last made the journey. A short break, there and back in a flash, much enjoyed and appreciated, but soon to slip into memory with other loved and appreciated breaks. Gone, but never quite forgotten, always there in the recesses of your brain and one day surfacing like a bitter-sweet ache through your heart. If only, yes if only there was a way of going back. Walking up and down the platform of Herne Hill Station: two red brick buildings, one of them a waiting room. The other one closed with a stand of soft drinks, etc. that can be seen through the window. Obviously meant to be a station café, a project started and aborted, or a café closed down for lack of customers. Leena doesn't know.

She hasn't checked the train times. Having established that trains to Luton are quite frequent, she has simply given herself enough time, calculating that she might have to wait at Herne Hill for a while. It turned out she arrived with only five minutes to spare, so no long wait. After four minutes, the notice board showed that the train had been delayed by ten minutes. Never mind, she had the time.

It was late February. Crossing the Thames, passing Alexandra Palace in the distance, like a fairy-tale castle. Then the flat English landscape...details of the train ride disappear. She remembers the two pyjamas bought at M&S for the occasion, one purple and one navy, pure cotton, still going strong, a tangible link to a happier past. In view of the present crisis her whole life is a happier past.

In her mind Herne Hill has become the gateway to Budapest.

Distant memories now. Like something that happened in a different life. Sitting in her suburban house, Leena finds it hard to believe that there was a time when she visited Budapest several times. Her very first evening there, going for a stroll with Sam while Aurora was finishing the meal. A few streets and they were on the banks of the river Danube. In front of them Freedom Bridge luminous green in the dark. The silent river flowing below, wide and swift, shimmering under the lights of the city, dreamlike and other-worldly.

In the days to come, and on subsequent visits, crossing the Danube, walking along the Danube – a river she had known about since childhood, first encountered in *the Beautiful Blue Danube Waltz* by Johann Strauss...Going to Margit Island in the Danube, once to a magnificent

41

outdoor concert with three tenors, and once, in summer, just to walk around admiring the flowers, stopping to enjoy the musical fountains with water cascading high up in the air, moving and dancing with the music. On a winter's day she made her way there on her own, walking past a little zoo she hadn't come across before. It was a cool and misty day, and apart from a handful of dedicated walkers, she was the only one around. The zoo was closed and deer came right up to the fence to say hello. They went to a magnificent opera house, all baroque opulence and gold leaf, to see the ballet, Manon. Many times, she walked past the synagogue that looked like a mosque, an impressive building of yellow brick. She bought fruit and vegetables in the enormous indoor market, housed in an ornate construction by the Danube. During the day she and Sam went to pleasant little cafés. Being a writer, he liked to work in cafés. In the evenings the three of them went to ruin bars, quite a few of them in Budapest – where somebody has thought of setting up a bar in the ruins of an old building. Pleasant, not very well-lit spaces, mainly young or youngish clientele, but not only. Leena loved it there.

Even the block where Sam and Aurora lived had a magic of its own, or rather of its kind. A typical Budapest block, built in the late 19th century around an inner courtyard. A walkway runs around each floor from which people enter their flats, much like the walkways you see on British council blocks, only in Britain the walkways are on the outside, facing the street rather than circling the inside. Sam and Aurora's flat was on the third floor.

Very high ceilings, windows facing the inner courtyard with the walkways.

There was one Saturday night when they were going out. It was dark. Piano music emanating from one of the flats. Somebody was playing a Chopin waltz, and doing it well. The sorrow-sweet waltz followed them down the stairs, growing fainter, until it could no longer be heard. Was this the night when they were off to an Indian restaurant? No, it couldn't have been, this must have been during her February visit, as it was dark. They went to the Indian restaurant in summer. She is sure of it because she remembers wearing light clothes. In all of Budapest there are only one or two Indian restaurants. This one was a fair metro-ride away, and an attractive establishment. A polite Indian waiter escorted them to their table and handed them their menus. They immediately became aware of three British men at the next table, large beer glasses in front of them, no food as yet, half-drunken shouts and laughter, impossible to keep up a conversation. When the waiter appeared with their drinks Aurora asked in Hungarian if they could move to a different table, as the three men were being annoyingly noisy. The waiter nodded. However, he did not escort them to a different table, he just went out. Shortly after he returned with another waiter or perhaps the manager. The three men were told to leave, angry and offended they objected loudly, but to no avail, they had to go.

There is no doubt that Budapest has got everything that is needed to be described as a beautiful city ... wonderful old buildings, a variety of parks, spas, opera houses, ornate cathedrals and castles, beautiful bridges spanning a fabled river ... But there is something more, a certain "je ne sais quoi" that comes with age-old civilisation and culture. Somehow London hasn't quite got it, neither has Oslo, but Prague has ... something indefinable, not even like the difference between old money and new, it's more subtle, yet you will recognise it when you see it. At least some people will. Cities where a more genuine heart is beating. Cities where 21st century materialism has not yet taken hold.

Sitting in her house in humdrum suburbia it is hard to believe that not so long ago, she knew her way around Budapest, at least a section of it. Strange to think that it is still there. If it hadn't been for the damn virus, she could have gone there tomorrow and found everything as it was when she left it, give or take a few minor changes, like a café having a new owner, or new buildings having sprouted here and there, but basically things would be the same. Notwithstanding the biggest change of all ... Sam no longer lives there.

Leena's dearest wish is to book a ticket to Budapest, and make one of her journeys all over again. If only we could return to the past, and stay there.

March 24th, 2020

From her bedroom window Leena would look across to Norwood Tower, standing tall on a hill, from a distance much like the better-known Crystal Palace tower, a landmark which in turn looks like the Eiffel Tower. At night the whole of Norwood Tower is studded with red lights from top to bottom. Before going to bed, Leena would always stop at the window and contemplate it, thinking that over there, under the watchful eye of the red tower, was little Amelia, fast asleep.

Yesterday Britain went into complete lockdown.

"You must stay at home."

Boris Johnson locks down Britain – shutting shops and churches, banning weddings and forbidding meetings of more than two people in toughest yet – German-style – coronavirus lockdown.

Boris Johnson announces the most draconian lockdown in British peace or wartime history: People are banned from leaving home except for food, medical treatment, ONE exercise per day, or essential work … or the police will FINE you.

PM said that for at least three weeks people should only go out for essential goods, or brief exercise. Britons should only travel to and from work if it is absolutely necessary and it cannot be done from home. No visitors allowed in your home, not even close family members.

People knew it was coming and a lot of people, like Leena, had been more or less self-isolating for some time. But now it was definite. The measures that seemed so inhumane when Leena read about them in her friend's Facebook post from Vienna, were upon them, announced yesterday evening in Boris Johnson's talk to the nation. Even so, this morning's rush hour saw people cramming into Tube trains the same as always. On Sunday, because of the truly beautiful weather, people hungry

45

for sunshine after a long, dark and wet winter flocked together in parks and on beaches, rubbing shoulders, breathing each other's recycled air. Some people simply refuse to get it. Others – those are the pitiable ones – cram into overcrowded Tubes and buses because they have no other way to get into work, if not they stand to lose their jobs. Without a job, no money, and soon they might be homeless.

*

2:40 on a Tuesday afternoon, the time Tom and Leena would leave to pick up Amelia from the child minder. Their car had no child seat, so Tom would deposit Leena outside the childminder's. Sometimes he would drive straight home, other times he would drive to Allan's street and wait in the car for Leena and Amelia to arrive. He would stay with them in the flat for an hour or two before driving home on his own. Leena, on the other hand, would enter the child minder's house to find three or four little ones toddling round, Amelia happy to see her. Leena would dress her, put her in the buggy and off they'd go. This Tuesday routine went on for nearly three years, at first picking up Amelia from the child minder, and after her second birthday, from a nursery just under Norwood Tower, a short walk from her home. As Amelia got older, and weather permitting, they would stop in the park near her home. Amelia would have a snack Leena had brought for her, and feed the ducks in the lake. In summer, they would buy ice-cream from the man in the kiosk.

Back in the house, Leena would look after Amelia until either Allan or Elida returned from work between 7 and 8pm. She would stay and chat for a short while before getting a cab home where Tom would be waiting. Leena gave up on driving 20 years ago, and Tom was slowing down, unnoticeably at first, then more rapidly. More often than not he would come up with excuses not to drive. When Leena got home, Tom would be in front of the TV. Sometimes Leena would heat up ready-made fish and chips from M&S for the two of them, other times Tom would already have had his dinner, having bought himself an Indian takeaway and had the good sense to order enough for Leena as well.

And one fine spring... three weeks' illness, and Tom was no more. Sam was living in Budapest, and Leena continued to pick up Amelia from the nursery every Tuesday afternoon for another year and a few months. But then, that ended too, when Allan took his family to live on Grand Cayman.

Time moves on. Leena was writing and going to her choir. Uneventful weeks interspersed with visits to Norway, Budapest and Grand Cayman, and subsequently Berlin. Looking back, it feels like the Tuesday routine went on for a long time even though it was only around three years. With Tom gone, Leena would take the bus to Chrystal Palace and walk to Amelia's nursery from there. Rather than waiting for a bus, she would take a cab home.

She couldn't help wondering how her family could have disintegrated so completely in a couple of years. She thought life as she knew it would go on forever, and yet, here she was, alone, in a country which, after all, was not her country. Sam returned though, and moved to Walthamstow. Often, on a weekend, she would make her way across London to see him. They had some wonderful Sunday walks around the Walthamstow Marshes and the River Lee, stopping at a small café by the river for a snack and a cup of tea. Walking along they would see the Hasidic Jews of Stamford Hill, also out on a Sunday afternoon walk. The men with their long side curls and large fur hats, white stockings, black knickerbockers and black coats. The women with hats atop their wigs, wearing old-fashioned navy coats, skirts well below their knees, like something out of the 1950s…Lots of children, some boys racing around on bikes like boys everywhere. The girls were more demure, practicing for a career as obedient housewives, not yet following the strict and modest dress code, letting their hair flow freely. Married women have to cover their hair, usually with a wig. Or, they shave their heads, because you cannot accidentally show the hair you haven't got. Groups of one or two families walking together, like flocks of alien birds with an invisible wall between themselves and the rest of the Sunday walkers. Apparently, the largest community of Hasidic Jews in Europe. Leena finds them fascinating—the way they have managed to keep their culture and ethnicity alive without a country to call their own, sticking to themselves and their customs—a foreign body in mainstream cultures, often causing resentment. You see them on the Victoria Line as well. Mostly women who have been shopping on Oxford Street. Do the Hasidic Jews of Stamford Hill speak

Yiddish among themselves? Even when coming up close on the Tube, Leena has never managed to grasp which language they are speaking. Apparently, before World War II there were 13 million Yiddish speakers in Europe. Now there are estimated to be around 2.5 million. Over the years Leena has had and still has Jewish friends, but always of a secular persuasion.

Leena would not want the restricted lives of Hasidic Jews, but she enjoys seeing them – something exotic and different that you never see in Norway. When she was growing up you hardly ever saw anyone who was not an ethnic Norwegian. She remembers a Swiss painter/decorator, and an Italian family that lived quite close by. Neither looked sufficiently different to stand out in a crowd. People of more distant cultures and religions were by and large unheard of. Before world War II, however, there were quite a few Jewish people living in Norway. During the German occupation some made it across the border to Sweden, but the majority ended up in Hitler's death camps. Only a handful came back.

A memory springs to mind: Leena was 20 years old. Her father's brother, Oluf, who had emigrated to Canada as a young man, and his Canadian wife, Caroline, were spending a couple of weeks with them. Leena and her father drove them to the Westcountry where the two brothers had grown up, a trip the family had done every summer for years. Driving through the tiny town of Nordfjordeid, they passed a cemetery where the head-stones were close together, almost on top of each other, and Auntie Caroline remarked: "Look, there's a Jewish cemetery."

Leena replied: "No, no! It's only an ordinary Norwegian cemetery."

Caroline: "Are you sure it's not a Jewish cemetery?"

A Jewish cemetery in a small Norwegian town in the middle of nowhere ... unthinkable.

The fact that such a cemetery was an impossibility, brought home to Leena that she did indeed live in a limited society where everybody was basically the same. Most of her compatriots, however, would have been proud to say, "Oh no, we only have proper Norwegians here." They liked their homogenous society; indeed, they preferred it. It was safe, they knew where they stood. They knew the social codes. Things have changed now, with an influx of immigrants and refugees from developing countries. Most ethnic Norwegians resent them; they liked things the way they were. Consequently, the country has some of the strictest immigration laws in the world.

But Leena was different. She thought people from other countries were exciting.

*

The first day of lockdown is grinding its way towards evening. It is 4pm. The sky is still without cloud. In a minute Leena will be going out for her permitted one exercise walk a day. It is not the Walthamstow Marshes and exotic-looking people are few and far between, but it is green, and in parts quite beautiful.

March 26th, 2020

Strange times. Very little traffic. People walking past her house that would normally be at work. All non-essential shops are closed; only chemists and supermarkets are open, and the so-called post office housed in an off-licence some 10 minutes' walk away. Onal, her next-door neighbour came to her door and said he was going shopping, and did she need anything? Nice people. Onal is a Cypriote and the wife, Andrea, is from Slovakia. At the beginning of lockdown Leena had promised Allan and Sam to stay away from shops. Consequently, she had been wondering how to keep up her supply of fruit and vegetables. She wrote Onal a list, taking care only to mention things that were easy to find.

*

The Prince of Wales has tested positive for coronavirus, believed to have caught the disease when shaking hands with Prince Albert of Monaco two weeks ago.

He has been displaying mild symptoms but otherwise remains in good health and has been working from home for the last few days.

The Duchess of Cornwall has also been tested but does not have the virus. In accordance with government and medical advice, the Prince and the Duchess are now self-isolating at home in Scotland.

The Queen is said to be in "good health" and is still following all appropriate guidance after her son and heir was diagnosed.

*

Yesterday Leena's friend Gunilla, sent her an article on the concept of "viral load". Leena forwarded it to her friends:

Viral load!

Why do we need to shut places where people group together? Because of VIRAL LOAD:

The amount of virus in your blood at the first infection, directly relates to the severity of the illness you will suffer.

So, if you are in a pub or religious building or entertainment venue with 200 people – and a large number don't have symptoms – but are shedding the virus, you are breathing in lots of droplets per minute and therefore absorbing a high load of the virus. Three days later you wonder why you can't breathe and end up in hospital. You had decided, because you were young and healthy, it wasn't going to be a problem.

Because the elderly are isolating quite well, the initial UK data suggests that all age groups above 20 are now almost equally represented in ITUs in England. Most of the cases are in London but the wave is moving outwards. This means that being under 60 and fit and well does not seem to be as protective as we thought. It seems that too many Londoners did not do as asked, but congregated in large groups in confined spaces and got a large initial viral load. They then went home and infected their wider families. Which is why London is overwhelmed.

No medicines will help this process meaningfully, hence there is no "cure" for this virus.

The same as with any bacteria or virus. Everybody knows that if you spend time in a room with several people coughing and sneezing you are likely to catch their colds, but less likely when coming across one person with a cold. There is a lot to be said for good old-fashioned common sense.

*

Yesterday Patsy, another friend and neighbour, texted Leena saying that she and her husband, Mike, were going to the early opening at M&S especially for people over 70 and health workers. A slightly controversial mix as health workers are more likely to be carrying the virus than other groups. However, there have been tragic scenes in the evenings when health workers have turned up late because of their shifts and found nothing but empty shelves. At least in this way they are able to get supplies.

Patsy and Mike returned with milk, satsumas, blueberries and eggs, which was what Leena had asked for. They have their own worries. Their daughter, Karen, is a doctor, an obstetrician. She and her husband were on holiday in Canada. Knowing it would be her last chance for a holiday until God knows when, they took this chance for a break. They got back on Monday and Karen went straight to work. Next week she'll be redeployed to work with corona victims. They all hope she'll be given proper protective gear, of which some hospitals have run out completely. A scandal if ever there was one, showing the government's inability to handle the situation.

*

Amelia called her on Facetime. She does it herself from time to time. She and Leena became very close during the years when Leena regularly looked after her. She is a sensible girl. She told Leena that she'd been supposed to go to a friend's birthday party but couldn't go because of corona. Amelia's birthday is on the 4th of June. She hopes that by then everything will be back to normal so she can have her party. But even if she can't have a party with her friends, she can still have a party with Mummy and Daddy and Lea.

*

And in Spain 655 people died overnight, bringing the death toll to over 4,000. An ice rink in Madrid has been converted into a morgue.

March 27th, 2020

This is totally horrendous: *Spain's coronavirus deaths spike to 4,856 after 769 die from the rapidly spreading disease.*

Boris Johnson has tested positive and has self-isolated in Downing Street. He is working from his room and his meals are left outside his door. From his office he sends out messages that he is well and continuing to run the country thanks to technology.

Health Secretary Matt Hancock has tested positive as well.

Britain's chief Medical Officer has coronavirus. Chris Whitty says he has been hit by symptoms just hours after Boris Johnson and Matt Hancock both test positive for the killer virus.

Government is mauled over coronavirus testing failures as the disease strikes down Boris Johnson, Matt Hancock and Chris Whitty – the three men leading the country's response to the virus. Now all of Westminster is wondering – who is next?

Why didn't they practice what they preached?

March 28th, 2020

When Leena woke up in the small hours, it was still dark. "One of those nights," she thought, as she switched on her bedside lamp to look at her watch. It had been a nuisance for years – waking up between 3 and 4 in the morning, fully alert and ready to face the day. Usually she would remain awake for a couple of hours, with brilliant ideas and solutions to her own and the world's problems racing through her mind. Ideas that would fade in the cold light of day, showing themselves for what they were – the figments of an overactive imagination. Most nights she would go back to sleep around 6 o'clock. When she was working, this broken sleep routine was a real problem, for no sooner had she drifted off to sleep again, than the alarm would wake her up. Feeling tired and groggy, she would get up and get ready for work. If this happened two nights in a row, she would be quite exhausted by Thursday, which was the end of the teaching week and a day that felt like a slog at the best of times. Her schedule was such that on Thursdays she had a two-hour lecture from 10 till 12, and then nothing until 3pm. There was plenty of work to get on with, so she wasn't twiddling her thumbs, but struggling to stay awake. She dearly wished she had a sofa to lie down on. She knew she was in trouble, when come 2 o'clock, she would rush across to the university shop for a big Mars bar and make herself a mug of strong coffee in her office. From being a skinny child, she had matured into a woman who needed to watch her figure.

Early October 1993

Leena was on her way to her new position at University College London. Excited, apprehensive, happy, hopeful. After years of freelance work combined with childcare and domestic duties, she had made it. Finally. She had served her apprenticeship, and here she was.

Was it her first teaching day in her new job? It might have been, but she can't quite remember. Too long ago now. She was on the Victoria Line, from Victoria to Warren Street. The carriage was fairly crowded and she was standing near the door. That was when a woman sitting a couple of seats away from her caught her eye. A Slone ranger if ever there was one. You don't see many Sloane rangers on the Tube, at least not on this stretch, because Sloane rangers live in Kensington or Chelsea and get about in classy little cars. But there she was – mid-40s, a perfectly groomed reddish-blond bob, fine aristocratic features, elegant orange-brown jacket, white shirt, long amber necklace, smart dark trousers, a worn leather briefcase on her lap, incongruous among scruffy Londoners and tourists in jeans and T-shirts. What was Leena wearing? Most likely a flowery Indian skirt and a red cotton jumper. An outfit she often wore that autumn – she remembers it well – cheap and cheerful like all her clothes in those days because it was all she could afford. The train arrived at Warren Street. Leena got off, and the smart Sloane ranger slipped out of her mind.

She was half way through her first lecture of the day when the fire alarm went off. The staff knew it was a drill, but the students had no idea, as far as they were concerned it might well be real.

They had been instructed to shepherd their students out through the back door and to wait for the all clear in the inner court yard. And there, right in the middle of staff and students milling about, stood the stylish Sloane ranger from the Tube, still incongruous among casual-looking students and unglamorous academics. How utterly bizarre!

As the years rolled by, Leena's enthusiasm began to wane, and the work, that had so enriched her life, became more of a struggle than a pleasure. Especially on Thursday afternoons, when she would paste a smile on her face and force herself to look upbeat as she approached the classroom for a two-hour stint with the first years, the final teaching hours of the week. The Sloane ranger, who was not a Sloane ranger at all, but a German lady, Renate, who lived, not in a super-expensive town house in Chelsea, but in an ordinary house not far from Leena, was already at her desk teaching. Renate had been in the German Department for a good few years before Leena came on the scene in the Department of Scandinavian Studies. From speaking briefly in the corridor, they gradually became friends. There was an affinity; although different in many ways – Leena was an introvert. Being on the go, and with people all the time, exhausted her. Whereas Renate thrived on 'being out there' as she put it, squeezing in a coffee with a friend after work, before rushing off to a lecture somewhere. But they understood each other. Similar interests, similar backgrounds back home, both married to what Renate called OGs, Oriental Gentlemen. Renate's husband being Jewish and Tom being Egyptian. Also, they both had two sons. Renate was teaching at another university as well, and only worked at UCL from 3-5 on Thursdays. Leena always felt such relief when she saw her through the window in her classroom door. It signalled the longed-for end of the working week. Only two hours to go, and then freedom until Monday, not counting marking and preparation. At 5 they would often meet up and go to the university café for a piece of cheese cake and a cappuccino.

They both loved music. Sometimes they would go together to a classical concert, and Renate was a faithful guest when Leena's choir held a concert, and she would always bring friends with her to help boost audience numbers. Living fairly close to each other, they were no strangers to each other's homes.

Nothing lasts for ever. Renate lost her long battle with cancer on November 11th 2019. A lot more could be said about her, fiercely intelligent, interested in everything, elegant and upbeat till her final day. She was going to start some experimental treatment, in an attempt to slow down the cancer and buy her a few more months. She wasn't ready to leave her sons and grandchildren quite yet. One afternoon in early October she popped by Leena's house with three books she thought Leena might like to read, still glamorous in navy jeans and a smart pale-blue jacket, white polo-neck jumper and a long blue necklace. But she was painfully thin. They had tea and talked mainly about Brexit, which they were both dead against. Renate didn't want to eat anything because food no longer agreed with her, not even a dry biscuit. She loved her work. After 20 years, Leena had had enough and left to pursue other interests, but Renate had soldiered on. She had only recently informed the university that she would not be returning.

Leena never saw her again. A few days later Leena went to Berlin for a couple of weeks. When she returned, Renate was in hospital, too ill for visitors. The new treatment had not been successful, it only made her feel awful, so they stopped it. Five weeks after bringing Leena the books, Renate was no more.

*

On this particular morning Leena was relieved to discover that it was already 20 to 5. She went back to bed where she remained awake until the contours of furniture and pictures began to emerge from the shadows, and it was time to get up, for another day in lockdown.

March 29th, 2020

The sky is white. She often wondered why on some days the sky looks white rather than blue, even though there is not a cloud to be seen. She asked Anita, her astronomer friend, and was told that it has to do with a thin layer of ice crystals, called cirrostratus cloud, that has formed some 6,000–13,000 metres up in the atmosphere, and is shielding the earth from the heavens above like a translucent blanket. Somehow, Leena likes the white sky, it makes the world look stagnant, which in these days of isolation indeed it is. The magnolia tree outside her window has lost many of its pink flowers and looks less striking against the white sky than against the blue. It is developing buds that will soon turn into a new season's growth. Our lives have changed, but nature continues as though nothing untoward has happened.

Having the time and opportunity to sit and watch the changing colours of the sky, all day long if you like, would not have been such a bad thing if only the reasons for being able to do so had been less worrying. A lower bank of white cloud has sailed up to cover the crystalline sky, and an icy wind is shaking the fragile branches of the magnolia tree. A cold and unfriendly day.

*

When your days are without content and the future is too uncertain for plans, the only way to look is back. And today a memory from the summer of 1957 cropped up in Leena's mind, partly crystal clear, and partly shrouded in mist.

They travelled a lot that summer. Much more than their yearly visit to her father's family in the West. They had driven all the way through southern Sweden to Copenhagen, with Leena avidly watching the passing landscape expecting it to change as soon as they crossed the border into Sweden, and feeling disappointed when it remained exactly the same. The big treat was that Hans' girlfriend, Dora, was coming with them. She was so beautiful, her hair quite long, somewhere between light-brown and honey. She was tall, 175 centimetres, almost as tall as Hans. Green eyes. Once, when she came to visit, she had a lovely chiffon scarf tied round her hair, like a hairband. It was a colour Leena had never seen before. She asked Dora what it was called, and Dora replied that it was turquoise, which is neither blue nor green, but somewhere in between.

They bought food in a small Swedish town, which her mother cooked on a portable gas stove. For their first meal on the road, Berit had bought a thick sausage of a type she remembered from living in Sweden in her youth. She sliced it and fried it in the frying pan. They ate it with boiled potatoes and that was all. Delicious. They spent the first night in a hotel in Gothenburg, with her mother, Dora, Leena and John sharing a room, and Hans and her father sleeping in a different room. No bathroom, only a white wash basin in their room with soap, white towels and hot and cold water. Berit and Dora talking about men's filthy habits—always leaving the wash basin grimy instead of rinsing away the residue when they'd finished washing. When they had all washed and changed into smarter clothes, they met up with her father and Hans and went to Liseberg, a famous theme park where Leena saw a roller-coaster for the first time in her life. She remembers it careering up and down and people shrieking and laughing, but that is all she can recall from her first and only visit to Liseberg. After a while the parents took their kids back to the hotel, but Hans and Dora stayed on. They had even gone on the roller-coaster.

The following day – driving through Sweden in their Dodge, a huge car that her father had bought in America and had shipped over to Norway, green with seats in a fine multicoloured material. So roomy that Leena and John could almost play hide and seek on the backseat. Dora, Leena and John in the back. Hans was 18 and had a fresh driving licence, as had her father. Out of the two, Hans was the better driver, and there was some bickering as to who should be driving, even though they took it in turns. Leena can't recall where her mother was sitting, most likely in the back with them, but she can't remember and little does it matter, trying to squeeze out the memory is doing no good at all. But she remembers the flat landscape of southern Sweden and here and there a windmill, sometimes close, and sometimes further away. She had never seen a windmill before.

Leena has few memories from Copenhagen. They stayed in a hotel that her mother thought was much too shabby, but it was all they could find as it was the holiday season and everything was booked up. She remembers seeing a donkey pulling a cart, the first donkey she had ever seen, and in a shop window they saw a television set, a miracle that had yet to arrive in Norway. They couldn't have stayed more than a couple of days. One day they went to the zoo. There was no zoo in Norway, so this was exiting. She especially recalls a wolf, very sad-looking, pacing up and down its naked 20-metre-long cage. Leena was wearing a red pleated skirt and a pale-blue angora jumper with short sleeves. She remembers the outfit well. No memory of what the others were wearing except that the two women wore smart dresses, her mother's possibly navy and white with a pencil skirt. Leena remembers a dress like that, and with a hat, shoes, gloves and handbag in white. And Dora...Leena can't remember. She had a navy dress with a full skirt and yellow polka-dots, so perhaps that was it. The men must have been wearing suits. There was a black and white photo which has since been lost of Leena and John sitting on a donkey in the zoo. Leena in her pleated skirt and John in short trousers and what looks like a T-shirt. The people in the background were all dressed up for the day, the men in smart trousers, shirt and tie. No jackets. Leena remembers it was sunny. A time when people dressed up for a day at the zoo.

Later that summer they did their yearly drive to the West, but only Leena and John and their parents.

After that there was a second trip to Sweden. Looking back, Leena can't for the life of her remember where it fits into the picture. It must have been in connection with a visit to her uncle and auntie who had just moved to Halden, a small town near the Swedish border. Being so close to the border, they had probably made a foray into Sweden. Leena remembers stopping at a kiosk for hot-dogs. She wanted to bring something home with her as well. Looking at all the unfamiliar sweets on offer, and with her parents shouting at her to hurry up, she opted for a bag of red and white sweets that turned out to be crumbly mints. Not bad, but she could have done better if they had given her more time to choose.

It was dark as they drew up in front of the house. Light in every window. Loud music, the type that had never been played in that house before. They had a stack of records, mainly classical plus a few tangos and some children's records, nice enough, but this music was something else. Heady, a different world, young, lively. In their absence, which couldn't have been more than a few days, the house had undergone a transformation. With the sedate older people and their kids gone, the two 18-year-olds, and very likely their friends, had transformed the atmosphere of the house and filled it with the intoxicating vibrations of youth, sex and laughter. Leena felt it the minute she set foot inside, although, she could not have put it into words – not at the age of eight.

It didn't last. Hans and Dora left soon after they arrived, and by the time the adults and two children sat down to supper, the house was back to its demure and quiet self.

School had already started. Leena's teacher, Miss Johansen had left to teach at a bigger and better school in Oslo. She was not related to Mr Johansen who kept the class in check for three years until the bright kids,

Leena included, went to Middle School in Hønefoss, and the not-so-bright kids stayed on for another year, with girls doing mainly domestic science and needlework and boys doing mostly woodwork. Their new teacher, Miss Tronrud, was kind, but she was very young and parents complained that she was not in the same league as Miss Johansen.

And so, Leena's memorable summer of 1957 faded into history to the tunes of *Oh Mein Papa*, *Jailhouse Rock* and *Wake up Little Suzie*. The music didn't last either. The records soon returned to Dora's home where they belonged. Hans was around, but he didn't much figure in the lives of his younger siblings. Either he was in his room doing school work – it was the final year of his baccalaureate – or he was off seeing Dora.

The nights were drawing in. And with the waning summer, Hans' and Dora's youth was drawing to a close before it had properly started. In February they were married, and a few months later their twin boys, Olav and Willum, were born. Hans' plans to become an airline pilot were shelved, and he found himself on building sites in Oslo learning to become an electrician. Two years later he disappeared without a trace. Their parents moved heaven and earth to find him, but to no avail. He was neither seen nor heard of for nearly sixty years. After an opportunistic vanishing act, he had lived out his life under a different identity. Much of his talent had gone into not being found. Once, he had rubbed shoulders with Leena in the Norwegian Church in London. Due to the likeness to their mother, and being the right age, he was pretty sure it was her. She, however, had been busy with her children and failed to notice the sailor standing close by, leafing through Norwegian newspapers laid out on a table.

Hans made a point of visiting the Norwegian church whenever his ship came to London, but he never saw her again.

March 31st 2020, 9pm Berlin time

Allan calls her on his way from his office walking through the empty streets of Berlin on lockdown–streets full of bars and restaurants and at this hour usually teeming with people. But now all the bars are closed and the streets are empty but for a few returning late like himself. He sends her two photos, one of a deserted platform on the U-Bahn, and one of a U-Bahn carriage, which he had all to himself. He doesn't like to go into his office and it feels weird as he is the only one there. But, with two children on leave from school and nursery, working from home is near impossible. It's mainly the little one who can't understand why Daddy isn't playing with her.

April 4th, 2020

A perfect spring day. The sky is blue. A day for a picnic, a day for the beach, a day for working in the garden. Leena's back garden needs a lot of work, but she doesn't like to be there, not when the ogre next door is out. He dislikes Leena. He had it in for Tom, spreading rumours that being Middle Eastern he could not be trusted. He prefers ogres like himself, angry people finding problems with everything and everybody. Chances are he'll start pestering Leena about the eucalyptus tree in her garden. He must be pushing 80, but the expression, "old and mellow", does not apply to him.

When Leena and family moved in, his front garden was sweet, natural paving stones, heather and rose bushes in patches in between. By the fence, separating the two properties, stood a gorgeous winter jasmine, exceptionally tall, covered in yellow blossom in spring. The back garden too was beautiful. Deep-red peonies and shrubs, some of them bearing sweet smelling flowers, all of them old, perhaps there since the houses were built in 1928, their scent wafting across the fence. The old lady, who had lived there for who knows how long, had tended them with loving care, but then she passed away and the ogre moved in. For a few years he left well alone. But then, one day, work men arrived. Roses, shrubs and peonies were unceremoniously torn up, left in a heap on the pavement and subsequently driven away. The winter jasmine was cut down and a plastic bag tied over the stump to stop it from ever growing back. Front and back were paved over, not with natural stone of varying shapes and sizes, but with ordinary red bricks, making it look like a stone desert. Neighbours watched in horror. Judging by the new-look garden, the ogre's heart had turned to stone; how else could he destroy such sweet beauty and replace it with bricks and mortar?

He did not often talk to his neighbours, and when he did, it was invariably to complain about something or other: Cats were making a mess in his garden. "I hate cats." The trees on the common were sucking too much moisture from the ground: "I hate trees." Foxes made their way through his property: "I hate foxes." A landscape gardener lived in the corner house next to the common. To the delight of neighbours and passers-by, he had planted daffodils and hyacinths around the nearest oak tree. The ogre complained to the council asking if this was allowed, and if so, would it be all right for him to grow vegetables on the common? The flowers came back year after year, long after the gardener had moved away, but the ogre never got to grow his vegetables. These days it is Leena's eucalyptus tree that's causing him grief, its roots are spreading under the turf in his garden and he wants it cut down.

This morning he was out at the back, scraping moss from between the bricks on the patio. Angry vibrations emanating across the fence.

But, a lovely day. She works in the front. The pansies she bought the day before lockdown are doing well in their pots. She would have loved to buy more flowers and compost, but the garden centre down the road is closed, not being essential to people's survival, so no chance of that now.

*

Among Native Americans there is a belief that turquoises have healing and spiritual properties, and that they even can protect you from evil. They are believed to stand for calmness and serenity. A wonderfully silky stone that, whether you believe in its magical properties or not, is bound to make you feel better in yourself.

According to Native Americans the earth is a living organism and all things on it are precious. Turquoises are no exception; they represent life, and are highly revered because they appear to have colour-changing properties. Factors such as the environment, light, dust, and skin acidity all play a role in how the stone appears to the eye. While most people picture it with a beautiful blueish-green hue, other variations exist such as white, light blue, yellowish-green and a copper colour. Colours that to Native Americans represent the hues of the earth – a reason why they find the stone so attractive and fashion it into spectacular jewellery. To many South-American tribes they were more highly prized than gold.

*

On one of the last normal days before lockdown, Leena went to the Ecuadorian jeweller in the High Street. With the coronavirus becoming ever more threatening, she felt that what she needed was a large beautiful turquoise, like the ones she had seen in Native American jewellery. She liked to believe that it might calm her anxiety and keep the virus from attacking her. The jeweller had several turquoise pendants, but they were all disappointingly small, nothing like the eye-catching stones she had imagined. She bought the biggest one she could find, unimpressive though it was, and has been wearing it ever since. It certainly cannot do any harm. That was the day she ran into Francine in the High Street. There was a time when they saw quite a lot of each other, but as often happens around London, lives change and friendships fizzle out for no special reason. These days she and Francine talk happily enough when, by chance, they meet in a shop or in the street, but they never seek each other out. Rather than standing in the street they decided to go to a café for a cappuccino and a croissant. Like so often, Francine did most of the talking...about herself, her sons, her work, never once did she mention the coronavirus. Still, it was nice enough meeting her and they sat chatting for about an hour. Two days later buying a piece of jewellery and an impromptu visit to a café would have been out of the question.

Meanwhile, Breaking News

Britain suffers its worst coronavirus crises as 708 die on one day taking the total to 4,313. Five-year-old child with underlaying health issues becomes Britain's youngest victim as Britain suffers worst day yet in coronavirus crisis including 40 with no underlying health conditions. But infections are stabilising says government expert.

Italy is still worse hit. In Bergamo Hospital 800 people died yesterday alone.

Unimaginable.

*

But today, looking out of the window, all appears as well as can be. Everything peaceful, everything normal. Young people jogging past, older people walking. Leena wants the house and garden to look spic-and-span for when Sam arrives. He worries about her being on her own. Ever since lockdown he has been wanting to do her shopping for her, and once he did, getting caught in the rush hour on his way home across London. Since then Leena has been adamant: "I do not want you to risk your life to bring me shopping!" But Sam insists. Allan has been trying to talk him out of it too. Today he's coming. A friend is driving him. Sam has a licence, but has never been interested in owning a car. Leena gave up on driving years ago, and only rents a car when she's in Norway. Sam has not given up on it, but being a struggling writer, he simply cannot afford to run one. Besides, cars don't interest him.

Leena is wearing her smartest jeans and her red, short-sleeved Ralph Lauren top that she bought for her leaving party at work nearly six years ago, and the turquoise pendant of course. She has mown the front lawn. The red tulips that come up every spring are especially glorious this year.

*

They are here. Loads of shopping. Three large plastic bags full, plus bottles of sparkling water, toilet paper and kitchen rolls, enough for months. The three of them carry everything into the house, two metres apart, asking Leena to keep her distance. No hugs, no physical contact. His friend is an attractive woman of 27, called Annabel, wearing a long red skirt and Doc Martens. Sam has talked about her often, and now she has offered to drive him across London. Leena immediately likes her. She had envisaged food left on the doorstep and exchanging a few words through the car window before their driving away. Instead Sam lingers, showing Annabel the house and garden while Leena is tidying everything away. Strictly speaking they shouldn't have come into the house, but Leena is too happy to see them to say anything. She can hear him chatting to Onal, next door, a likeable man of forty who couldn't be more different from the ogre on the other side. He and his wife, Andrea, befriended Leena before they'd even moved in. They have two daughters, same age as Allan's girls. Then Sam suggests going for a walk around the park. He has brought face masks and gloves for Leena. For the first time ever, she puts on a mask. Off they go, the three of them leaving the house closer together than prescribed. On the other side of the fence the ogre is glaring at them. Leena pretends not to notice.

It suddenly hit her. This is the day they were meant to have their spring concert. Funny how concert day, that used to be so important, now seems so unimportant that she'd forgotten about it altogether. It's a beautiful evening. The sky a clean pure blue, no fine layer of ice crystals between heaven and earth today. Walking with the two of them feels like a party or a major event, like the world is suddenly back to normal. How many times has she walked around the park? Hundreds and hundreds. She still does, on her own, to get her one exercise a day, but it feels dreary, an obligation, something she has to do to keep fit and healthy. She tries to vary her daily walks, sometimes around the common and through the tiny wood, once she walked along the alleyways running behind the back gardens, but they were full of rubbish and not very inspiring. Some days it's a joy simply to get out of the house and smell fresh air, other days it feels like a slog and she longs for the walk to finish, one more kilometre now, and she'll go home. It depends on her mood and the weather.

There is a large lake in the park and in the middle of it, an island where herons live. The lake is full of all manner of other birds too, even kingfishers, which Leena has never seen. The park is the suburb's claim to fame, and much more beautiful than you'd expect. There are black cormorants with their long, hooked beaks, sitting in trees, spreading out their wings to dry. Unlike with other waterfowl, water gets between their feathers, hence the need to dry their wings. Once Leena counted ten birds in the same tree, all sitting still with wings outstretched. There are Canada-geese and greylags, and Egyptian geese with their pink legs and gentle colours. Sam wonders if there are any mandarin ducks, and Leena takes them to the end of the lake where she knows they can usually be found, and there they are. Annabel has never seen such colourful ducks and takes several pictures – the males with their vibrant plumage, and the females – only coloured in shades of grey and a bit of white, not striking, but still beautiful, like a forget-me-not or an inconspicuous person, you need to look closely to see their beauty ... One pair is mating as they walk past, they separate shaking their feathers. Another male has his eyes on the female and tries to get her away from her mate. She doesn't want to know and sticks with her mate of a minute ago, or perhaps life-long partner, Leena doesn't know. What she does know is that once a male has had his way with a female, he loses his extravagant plumage and ends up looking like a female, until next spring.

The walk, wonderful as it was, only lasted for about an hour. And then Sam and Annabel are gone, waving as they drive off down the road.

April 5th, 2020. Breaking News

UK's coronavirus outbreak is set to overtake Italy and France: A worrying new graphic shows that three weeks since Britain hit 50 deaths, it is in danger of being in a worse state than those countries were at the same point. The number of deaths is up by 621 to 4,934 today, including 29 patients without underlying health conditions. This means Britain's deaths could dwarf France's and Italy's. The level of infections has risen sharply by almost 60 per cent, to 47, 806, dashing hopes that the rate of people getting the disease was starting to level out.

Coronavirus-hit Boris Johnson receives oxygen treatment in hospital amid warnings he has risked his health by working through illness 'like hero Churchill'—amid calls for him to hand over the reins to deputy Dominic Raab. The premier is still running a temperature more than 10 days after he was confirmed as having the virus. His hospitalisation was announced shortly after the Queen addressed the nation in a rare televised message.

And there she was indomitable as always, not a hair out of place, green dress, a matching brooch, her beloved pearls, just as we have been used to seeing her for as long as most of us can remember, except for the obvious signs of ageing.

She talked about people having lost loved ones to the disease, and the difficult times in which we find ourselves, "a time of disruption in the life of our country: a disruption that has brought grief to some, financial difficulties to many, and enormous changes to the daily lives of us all." She went on to say, "the attributes of self-discipline, of quiet good-humoured resolve and of fellow-feeling that still characterise this country, the pride in who we are is not a part of our past, it defines our present and our future." She told Britons to trust in the knowledge that better days lie ahead. It was a heartfelt and rallying speech ending with the words, "we should take comfort that while we may have more still to endure, better days will return; we will be with our friends again; we will be with our families again; we will meet again."

Breaking News

*Mounting fears for Boris Johnson as PM **still** has a 'persistent cough and temperature' in hospital and Number 10 refuses to say if he is suffering from pneumonia – but claims he is in good spirits and still working. One MP suggests that he was too keen to emulate his hero, Winston Churchill, by defying the illness.*

Number 10 has announced concerns are mounting for Boris Johnson today as he remains in hospital, with Downing Street stating his symptoms are no longer 'mild'.

The 55-year-old was dramatically admitted to St Thomas', near Downing Street, last night after doctors raised alarm that his temperature has still not subsided 10 days after his positive test. Number 10 has insisted it was not an emergency admission and the premier remains in control of the government's response, despite staying in hospital with no clear timeframe for being discharged. However, his effective deputy, Dominic Raab chaired the daily coronavirus crisis committee meeting this morning, and full Cabinet tomorrow has been postponed. Experts say there is a risk of pneumonia when a temperature lasts more than a week. There have been claims Mr Johnson has been coughing heavily during conference calls. The PM's spokesman dismissed claims emanating from Russia that he is on a ventilator as 'disinformation'.

April 6th, 2020. Breaking News

Boris Johnson taken into intensive care. Mr Johnson was moved to the ICU at St Thomas' Hospital in central London and given oxygen last night after his health deteriorated sharply over just two hours, leaving doctors fearing he will end up needing a ventilator.

But the 55-year-old's spokesman claimed today: "The Prime Minister has been stable overnight and remains in good spirits. He is receiving standard oxygen treatment and breathing without assistance. He has not required ventilation or non-invasive respiratory support."

April 7th, 2020

Britain could be the worst coronavirus-hit nation in Europe with 66,000 deaths in the first wave of the outbreak – three times Italy's expected toll – because of NHS' shortage of hospital beds and intensive care capacity. The researchers forecast Britain will need 100,000 beds by mid-April to cope with the crisis, compared to the 17,765 currently available.

But the alarming projections do not take into account the thousands of beds that will become available in the new NHS Nightingale hospitals.

The number is also in stark contrast to predictions by the UK's leading scientific advisers, who warned around 20,000 people will die during the crisis.

April 10th, Good Friday

At about 3pm Leena decided to take her daily walk. To make it feel more like an afternoon in the park and less like exercise, she took with her a piece of carrot cake and a satsuma to be consumed on a bench. Six months ago, her Norwegian friend, Greta, had sent her a packet of cake-mix. Very easy to make, just mix in 200 mil cooking oil and two medium sized grated carrots. Leena wanted to keep it for a special occasion which somehow never materialised. Three days ago, sitting at home, not venturing to the shops and fancying something sweet, she remembered the cake-mix in her cupboard and thought; when is a special occasion if not now?

She would dearly have liked to go further afield, but shunning public transport, she is limited to where she can get to on foot, which mostly means the common and the park. The wide space of the common is impressive. Part of it borders a tiny wood, a remnant of ancient woodland. Some trees are old and gnarled, others are tall and leafy. Dense undergrowth – mainly impenetrable brambles. Several footpaths. A brook is running along the centre. From the wood you can cross a busy street and enter the park where she walked with Sam and Annabel. The park houses a children's playground with a café that sells ice cream, chips, coffee, and such like. Tables inside and out.

There is scope for variation. Some days starting with the common or the wood before entering the park, and some days vice versa. There are days when she doesn't feel like walking at all, and opts for only one or the other. Occasionally she ignores the green areas altogether and makes her way along suburban streets that have long since lost their attraction. When the world was normal, she preferred to go further afield. For example, she would take the train to London Bridge, walk through Borough Market and continue along the Thames past the Globe Theatre to the Southbank Centre. From there she would cross one of the Hungerford Bridges to Embankment and Charing Cross where she would catch a train home. On a Thames walk last September, her eyes were drawn to an elderly couple standing by the railings watching the river. They looked familiar. Then it dawned on her. It was Prunella Scales and Timothy West just standing close together, looking at the boats on the river. Leena had watched quite a few of their canal journeys in various parts of the world. With all those canal trips behind them, they must have had a lot of fond memories to think about. Leena stopped and stood a couple of metres away from them. Didn't look at them of course, it was simply nice to be in their vicinity. After about five minutes they continued their walk.

But today, like every day since lockdown, a local walk will have to do. First across the common where Sam ran one Mother's Day morning many years ago, he must have been 10 or 11. He wasn't in the house when they got up, but before they'd had time to wonder where he'd got to, he was back with a bunch of wild daffodils he had picked from the verge between the common and the road. The daffodils are still there, but not as plentiful as back then. Branches have fallen from trees. The grass is never cut ... Year by year the poor daffodils find their growing conditions ever less favourable. Some of them still cling on, and every time Leena passes, she thinks of a small boy, dressed in pale-blue jeans and a black coat with bright yellow lining, running out into the early morning to pick daffodils for his mother.

*

A beautiful afternoon, blue sky, sun filtered through delicate new leaves. The weather has been warm and sunny for days. You'd think it was the beginning of May, not the beginning of April. At least in this park you can still sit on a bench. Her friend, Clare, who lives in Walthamstow, not far from Sam, complains that the council has taped over all the benches to prevent people from using them.

Her next-door neighbours are doing noisy building work, and she can't even sit on a bench in the park and read to escape from the noise. The benches in this park have not suffered the same fate, but only one person per bench, and no sitting for too long. A policeman is walking about talking to people on benches. A young couple is sitting on the bench next to Leena's. The policeman says something to them. The woman replies that they have to sit there because they are musicians. The policeman doesn't understand what that has to do with anything. Neither does Leena. They explain, but Leena can't hear the explanation. They remain seated. Then it's Leena's turn. The policeman says to her, "I can see that you just got here, so that's all right, but don't stay too long."

Leena, cake in hand, "I'm only going to eat this, then I'll be on my way."

The policeman smiles, continues down a footpath and is gone. The young couple leaves, not a musical instrument in sight.

The cake is lovely. As she's not going to the shops, she is doing her best to make it last, one slice per day. Part of it is in the freezer to keep fresh. Leena has never been much of a baker. Now could be the time to improve her skills, but it doesn't appeal to her, it's too fiddly.

Across the lawn is the children's playground and the café where she used to take Amelia. On one of the family's visits to England, the two of them went to the playground. Amelia was hungry and Leena bought a large plate of chips for them to share. Amelia wanted a hotdog as well. Leena thought; she'll never eat it, but she did, gobbled it all up. Allan and Elida are strict about their children's diet. It should be healthy–very little salt, no additives, which is absolutely right. Leena is horrified to see what some parents regularly feed their children. Not expecting Amelia to eat much after the big hotdog, Leena put salt and ketchup on the chips. Amelia loved it, saying that this café has the yummiest chips. The first thing Amelia told her parents when she got home was, "I had chips with ketchup and salt." Never trust a four-year-old with a guilty secret.

An e-mail chimes on her mobile. It's from Sandy. They met at a creative writing class some 20 years ago and have remained in contact ever since. Tall and elegant, dark hair with streaks of grey, dressed in plain charcoal trousers and a white jumper, Sandy stood out from the rest of them. Married at 21 and with four children, whatever artistic and academic promise she might have shown, seemed forever lost. She'd never had a job. Still, buried deep inside was a secret wish to make something more of her life, and she joined the creative writing class. In her late 50s, she did a PhD in creative writing and subsequently branched off into painting and sculpture. A shining example that what you don't achieve in your youth, you can accomplish later. She and her husband are sitting out lockdown in their home in East Anglia, where they've been living for the last five years. She writes:

Thank you for your photo. It was cheering as I'd been seized with a feeling that the novelty of spring cleaning is wearing thin. We have an area of pamments in our house that never get cleaned–needless to say my art room is part of the area. (Leena doesn't know what pamments means, perhaps there is a typo somewhere). *My art room is so bad with layers of indecisiveness plainly obvious to the naked eye. I have thrown away a lot. Anyway, I washed the whole area (after a lot of hoovering and sweeping) and it's beginning to dry. The bits that are drying are cloudy and dull. I don't know why.*

The spring is scandalously beautiful through all this. I do hope this experience will change many, many things in this world. And New York is shocking … mass-graves … Who would have believed it?

It is lovely to just sit on the bench and Leena doesn't feel like continuing her walk just yet. The policeman is nowhere to be seen and it's not as though the park is full of people clamouring for her bench, so she might as well stay a while longer and reply to Sandy's letter:

Hi Sandy. So good to have this contact with you in these testing times. You said it, this spring is scandalously beautiful. Nature is rejoicing and putting on its best show, and hidden behind hospital walls in every country people are dying. I'm sitting on a bench in my local park, and everything looks normal. There are people about, but not many. They all look happy and relaxed. You'd think it's an ordinary Saturday. Suppose Good Friday amounts to the same thing. However, the playground and the café across the green are both closed and the ice-cream van that turns up every year when the weather warms up, has not appeared.

What can we do except stay away from people and clean our hands and our homes and be there for our family?

*

When Leena got home, she looked up pamments and discovered that it is a type of natural terracotta tiles. After nearly a lifetime in England, she still comes across things she's never heard of.

April 12th, 2020

The queen has called for 'light and life' to overcome despair amid the coronavirus crisis as she declared that Easter is 'not cancelled' in a special Bank Holiday message.

Her Majesty, 93, has delivered what is believed to be her first Easter address—which had one resolute message. The monarch's pre-recorded speech offered support to those marking Easter privately and the wider country. She said "by keeping apart we keep others safe" and added "we know that coronavirus will not overcome us."

Boy 11, with no underlying health issues becomes one of Britain's youngest corona victims as Covid-19 claims 917 lives in the last 24 hours—down from yesterday's record daily tally of 980—as new infections drop slightly too. But it does put Britain on course to hit the grim 10,000 milestone on Easter Sunday.

Berlin is a city where artists feel at home

Leena first came to Berlin with Tom in October 2013. Sam was living there on and off at the time and knew the city well and Tom was still in reasonable health.

A city, when you see it for the first time, slowly steps out of a mist of vague images and ideas, like a darkened room where the contours of pictures and furniture slowly emerge from the shadows as the night recedes and daylight takes over.

Tom and Leena stayed in a hotel by a large railway station, Hauptbahnhof, but Leena hadn't even noticed the name. Walk across the river Spree and across a wide green and you arrive at the Brandenburg Gate, the Reichstag with its huge dome and the Tiergarten.

Tom was not very well. Feeling tired, he spent a fair amount of time resting in the hotel room while Sam and Leena were out and about. Mostly in the Tiergarten, immediately behind the Brandenburg Gate—a large and truly magical park or rather forest—huge trees, pathways that seem to stretch on forever, making you forget that you are in the middle of a large city. It houses Berlin Zoo and there is a lake and a restaurant. However, Leena and Sam never made it to the lake or the zoo. Walking under the gigantic trees with their falling leaves was special enough. She went with Tom to the Jewish Memorial close to Brandenburg Gate—2,711 stone columns, all of them slightly different to represent the Jews killed in the Holocaust. Not much to look at, but as one walks deeper into it, one suddenly realises how oppressive the columns have become.

The three of them ate pizzas in restaurants, amazed at how cheap it was. They travelled about by tram and train, Sam leading the way. And everywhere they went the leaves were falling. Leena thought that whenever she'd think of

Berlin, she would see it through a veil of falling leaves, all of them yellow and all of them heart-shaped – the leaves of lime trees, dripping, floating through the air against a background of old apartment blocks painted red, yellow or green, like old buildings in Oslo. Often, they walked across a bridge where they looked down at disused railway tracks running across an area where nature had been allowed to take over.

Tom wasn't resting all the time. He and Leena made their way to Checkpoint Charlie. They took a disappointingly short boat trip down the Spree, and a tour of the city by bus, that somehow made very little impression on them. Leena remembers boarding the bus at the Brandenburg Gate. At one stage they came close to the tower she had noticed wherever she went – tall and slim with a glittering ball up high and with a slimmer extension on top of the ball – the TV Tower as it turned out, one of the GDR's prestige projects standing tall in the centre of Alexander Platz. Finally seeing it up close, Leena was hoping to get out and take a photo. But the guide, a young woman who looked like she'd rather be somewhere else, simply reeled off the facts from inside the bus:

The idea of an impressive TV tower mainly to broadcast GDR TV programmes was conceived in the early 1950s. However, work did not get under way until the 1960s. The design of a slender tower was created by GDR architect, Hermann Hanselmann. The sphere of the tower was intended to remind people of the Soviet sputnik satellites, and was to light up red, the colour of socialism. The construction consisted of an inner steel scaffold and an outer concrete shaft, which was erected around the steel scaffold. The total height is 365 metres; the ball, with a revolving restaurant is at 203 metres. Mounting the sphere at a height of 200 metres was a huge challenge. First the supporting steel frame of the sphere was prefabricated on the ground. The segments were lifted up with steel cranes and attached to the ring-shaped plat-form that form the final section of the concrete shaft ... With a flicker of interest, she added that when the tower was new, and the sun was shining, a cross appeared on the ball at the top. It kept appearing whatever the atheist authori-ties did to re-engineer it so it wouldn't happen.

Apart from the story of the TV Tower, Leena has only scant memories of the trip, caused by the disappointment of not getting out to have a proper look at the tower, and the boredom of travelling through areas of shiny modern blocks and shopping centres. They got similar lectures about some of the high-rise blocks, but by then Leena had switched off. She had expected old streets with character – to get a whiff of what might remain of pre-war Berlin with its thriving art and culture. Instead all she got was buildings of concrete and glass that could have been anywhere.

She thought the guide would have mentioned whether they were travelling through former East or West Berlin, but no such information came to light. As so often, it was a question of the eyes that see and the voice that tells the story. A more pragmatic person would have enjoyed seeing what a thoroughly modern city Berlin has become, and a different guide would have focused on things other than modernistic blocks and designer shops.

Only much later did she discover that many of the original streets are long gone. Back in 1938 Hitler had the idea to recreate Berlin as the magnificent capital of the Germanic empire he would be heading once he had achieved world domination. In other words, to construct a world capital comparable with Ancient Egypt, Babylon and Rome. His favourite architect, Albert Speer, was tasked with creating this new capital with avenues running from East to West and North to South. The reconstructed city would be renamed Germania, which would give all Germanic peoples and those of occupied countries of non-Germanic origin, a sense of national pride and identity. To this end many streets were dynamited. A small portion of the project was realised between 1938 and 1943, after which it was swallowed up by the war effort. Many more streets were annihilated by Allied bombing from 1944 till 1945. Hitler's dream of world domination ended with a bullet in his bunker on April 30th, 1945 with Allied troops hammering on his door.

These days the old streets can only be seen in pictures and museums such as the Märkisches Museum, or in reconstructions such as the TV series Babylon Berlin. The old streets, eradicated by Allied bombings and the dynamite of Albert Speer, are home to high-rise blocks, striking shopping centres and public buildings such as the magnificent Berlin Philharmonic Concert Hall.

*

On the Saturday morning Leena and Sam walked to a section of the Wall still standing, now covered in street art and called the East Side Gallery. With colourful murals painted by professional artists it no longer looked fore-boding at all.

Leena had one special wish, and that was to visit Kreuzberg, home to students, artists and a large Turkish community. Before the reunification it was part of West Berlin, but bordering the district of Friedrichshain which was in the East. She wanted to visit Kreuzberg because of the Norwegian novelist Dag Solstad, one of Norway's most acclaimed present-day authors, who had lived there back in the 1990s, in a flat overlooking the Turkish market and the Landwehr Canal. He describes the district in his novel 16.07.42, his date of birth. A strange title for a novel, but he must have had his reasons, or perhaps he couldn't think of anything else. A reflective, semi-autobi-ographical book. As always with this genre, it is difficult for a reader to know what is fact and what fiction without knowing the author personally. Leena enjoyed the book a lot, not so much for the descriptions of his wander-ings through Berlin, as for his failed school reunion in his native town in Southern Norway. He lived in Berlin at the time and had been taking part in a literature festival in Lillehammer. The end of the festival happened to coin-cide with the school reunion, which he was very much looking forward to. He had even invested in an Armani suit, and booked a room in the town's best hotel.

The eagerly awaited day arrived and in the late after-noon he made his way to the hotel where previous reunions had been held, expecting to find some of his old classmates already there. Nothing, the hotel was dead, no sign of an event taking place. He asked the receptionist. No, no such event today. Solstad promptly walked to a similar venue. Nothing. And so, he continued by taxi from one venue to the next, a couple of them well outside the town, thinking, I'll be too late for pre-dinner drinks, but I'll still make the starters. Then, I won't make the starters, but I should be in time for the main course ... Until he realised that he had missed the reunion altogether. Disheartened and hungry, he asked the taxi driver to stop by a kiosk where he ate a hotdog, standing by the roadside, in his Armani suit, before returning to his hotel room where he drank half a bottle of whisky. It turned out that the reunion was not held in an official venue at all, but in the flat of one of his classmates, which also happened to be the flat Solstad had grown up in. He had been so sure that the reunion would be in the same place as always that he hadn't bothered to read the invitation to the end. Leena likes the story because it is exactly the sort of mistake that she would make.

She saw him once, some ten years ago, around 6pm on a Sunday afternoon. It had been raining all day, and she had dropped in at Oslo's biggest news agent looking for a Norwegian crime novel that had just come out. And there he was – elderly, looking wild, wearing a navy cagoule and lighter coloured shorts, brown wellies nearly up to his knees. It had to be him. The right age, the characteristic hair, long, white and messy, exactly like in his photographs. Just the way Leena imagined him. A long day of concentrated writing, suddenly getting the idea that he needed to buy a paper, throwing on an anorak, sticking his feet in the enormous wellies, and off he went.

And there she was, one fine Saturday, walking along the Turkish market by the canal, looking up at the colourful blocks, thinking of the great author who had once lived behind one of the windows, and sat on one of the balconies, as described in his book.

*

As much as she liked Berlin, Leena did not expect to return. How could she have known that five years later she would be back, not with Sam, but with Allan and his family who had moved there during the spring of 2018. And stranger still, the disused railway tracks running across a deserted piece of land were next to their local station, Warschauerstraße. As the city slowly emerged from five-year-old memories and falling leaves, she learned that Allan and family lived in a district called Friedrichshain in former East Berlin, bordering the district of Kreuzberg. The bridge overlooking the disused ground was only a five minutes' walk from their flat. During communism, East Berliners had stood on the very same bridge gazing towards the unreachable West. And so, from the haze of falling leaves, a tangible city of cafés, restaurants, playgrounds and schools slowly came to life.

For two years the family lived in an old block, most likely late 19th century, perhaps slightly newer. No lift, making life difficult when you have to carry a child and heavy buggy up and down the stairs. It was a pleasant flat with high ceilings and a small balcony where you could sit and watch the goings-on in the street below. And what a lively street it was! Leena had never lived in a street like that and neither had Allan – full of bars, restaurants and small shops. Every flat surface covered in graffiti, some of it colourful and creative, deserving of the term street-art. Everywhere young and youngish people covered in tattoos – backs, legs, arms – some were beautifully drawn, but still mutilations, in Leena's opinion, a lifestyle statement that they can't get rid of. There is Boxhagener Platz, known to locals as Boxy, with its huge flee market every Sunday. The same people every week, unpacking and exhibiting the same old wares, once in a while selling an old coat, a vinyl record, a cup or two, glasses, jewellery, all kinds of bric-a-brac and tatt – paintings too; enough to keep their hopes alive. And, having a good time into the bargain. The park also houses a playground and a pad-dling-pool, so that during the week the district's children take over. Amelia loves it there. Not far away there is a red-brick church. It has since become known that it was a hotspot for counter revolution during the communist period, as were several of Berlin's churches.

The family has moved to a different flat since Leena's last visit. A new block in a more up-market part of Friedrichshain, some 15 minutes' walk away from the old flat. A modern third-floor apartment with two bathrooms; and three bedrooms: the girls sleeping in bunkbeds in one room and the third bedroom doubling as guest room and office/workspace. There is a working lift, which is a great blessing and a Lidl supermarket on the ground floor.

*

Today it's exactly two months since she embarked on her most recent trip to Berlin believing it to be one of many in 2020.

The plan had been for Leena to arrive at the new flat and then go with Allan to pick up Amelia from the Berlin Bilingual School and for the three of them to continue to collect Lea from her nursery.

However, the plane had been delayed so a new plan had to be hatched. Thank God for mobile phones and electronic communication. It was decided that she would take a taxi directly from Tegel Airport to Amelia's school and leave the taxi by the walkway where the children come out. For a while Leena had been worried about arriving in time for even that. But she made it just as the children and their guardians were emerging. Leena was looking for them when she heard a loud shout further down the walkway: "Nanny!" And, there they were, Amelia and Allan. Amelia wearing the same yellow coat and navy woolly hat as she had worn in London only a month ago. They returned to Berlin on January 6th, after spending ten days with Leena. She gave Amelia a bag of *Wotsits* that she had picked up on a whim in Sainsbury's back home, and on another whim stuck in her handbag as she was leaving for the airport. A good thing too. Back in England she used to bring Amelia a snack when picking her up from child-minder or nursery. So, all was well, Nanny had brought her a snack as she always did. Amelia gobbled up the *Wotsits* on the way to the station for the short tram ride to Lea's nursery. She practically licked the inside of the bag to get the last of the crumbs. If Leena had known she'd like them that much, she would have bought more. She had brought other things for Leena and Lea, but next time she would definitely bring more *Wotsits* as well. The plan was to be back some time towards the end of March.

Little Lea saw nothing strange or unusual about Nanny suddenly appearing with Daddy and Amelia. She trotted happily ahead of them, took off her slippers and got out her shoes. She knew exactly where to find her things. By the time they started on the walk to the new flat, it was already getting dark.

April 13th 2020

Grey sky. Leena woke up at 5 and heard the wind howling around the corners. Just as well, more in keeping with the traumatic times in which we find ourselves. Those hopelessly glorious days are in such a contrast to the misery that has descended on the world that it is almost indecent. She hasn't left the suburb for more than a month, and who knows when she'll get to leave it again. Out there, in every public space, the virus is lurking, so better stay put. Or can she just get on a train to London? Apparently, there are extra police constables at every station, asking people why they are travelling. If she has understood the restrictions correctly, she might be fined for being out and about without a good reason. Still, fine or no fine, she wouldn't want to risk her health by going there anyway.

It's two months ago to the day since she was in Berlin looking after Lea, taking her out in the morning, timing it so that she would start her midday sleep in her buggy. She was at the stage when she didn't quite need her day-time nap, but unable to go through the whole day without it, which meant that she would drop off much later in the afternoon and stay awake until 10-11 at night when her parents wanted some much-needed grownup time. A midday walk would rock her to sleep, whereas staying inside she would be wide awake until around 4. Leena knows it all from when Allan and Sam were little, always arranging her day to make sure they slept for a couple of hours to give her some time to herself. The worst thing was for somebody to turn up for a cup of tea just as she had got them off to sleep, robbing her of precious me-time, or rather, peace and quiet to get on with her translation work. It was a struggle, and when her fees finally arrived, it was invariably too little too late. With nearly five years between them, Allan was at school by the time Sam came along, so this routine, with a break in between, must have taken up close to four years of her life.

This morning Allan had taken Amelia to school before going to work. Elida was in bed. She really was not well at all. It had crossed Leena's mind that she might have caught the coronavirus, but obviously not. What she was displaying were classic flu-symptoms which were bad enough.

Near their old flat there was a pleasant Turkish café where Leena had taken both girls to eat cake during her visits. Leena would have a cappuccino and Amelia loved cocoa. Lea had apple juice. On her previous Berlin visit, Leena had given Lea a roll which she had bought on the way, plus bits of her cheese cake. Amelia was at school. Both girls clearly enjoyed going there. They sat nicely and quietly and were no trouble at all.

After they moved, however, this café was too far away. Leena discovered another one where she thought they could while away half an hour or so. But when they arrived every table was taken. Lea spotted some colourful cakes behind the glass counter – loads of pink buttercream and sweets and what-have-you on top. She pointed to them, but the assistant, a pleasant-looking Turkish lady, who knew a thing or two about toddlers and messy cakes, gave her a doughnut with chocolate icing instead, saying they could have three for the price of two. Having been given this far less glamourous cake by the lady, Lea neverthe-less accepted it, began eating and promptly dropped it on the floor. The lady was nice and gave her a new one. The doughnuts were lovely, very light and with only a thin coating of chocolate icing on top. And so, they walked back down the street eating their doughnuts. By the time they reached their block, Lea was fast asleep. Elida came out of her bedroom, took off her hat, coat and shoes and put her carefully to bed. On the one occasion when Leena had tried to do this, Lea had woken up, but sensing the feel of her mother she remained fast asleep.

Thinking about this day now, Leena would dearly like to go to a café, of which her suburb has many, for a cake and a cappuccino, or a ciabatta sandwich with brie and sun-blush tomato, sit for a while, perhaps run into somebody she knows, have a chat, maybe even stroll through the park together...But no, such simple pleasures are denied her, the cafés are closed. Besides she does not want to be in a crowded atmosphere, not now, but she always liked going to cafés...She's not complaining. She is alive and healthy. Thousands of people are not that lucky.

Still April 13th, 2020

Boris Johnson was discharged from St Thomas's Hospital this afternoon after a week of NHS treatment.

"Thank you for saving my life." Boris Johnson stops in Downing Street to deliver a tribute to the 'beating heart of this country', NHS, before heading with pregnant fiancée Carrie to Chequers by car to recuperate after a week in hospital, including three nights in intensive care.

Britain's coronavirus death toll surged past 10,000 today, marking a grim milestone in the country's epidemic.

The Writer in Abbey Road

There are many things that can make you feel guilty if you are so inclined. With Leena, one of them is bound up with her friend Renate.

It must have been at some stage during 2017 that Renate started talking about a German lady that she was visiting every fortnight or so. The lady was in her

90s, completely bedridden and lived in a flat in St John's Wood, North-West London. She had enjoyed an adventurous life living in Buenos Aires, Paris and Berlin, and presently London. Her name was Edith. Having spent large chunks of her life speaking Spanish, French and subsequently English, she now felt the need to speak German, her mother tongue until the age of 11, when her mother took her to live in Buenos Aires. Edith remembered Renate from when they had both attended lectures in the Goethe Institute and now Renate was visiting her to converse with her in German. How exactly this had come about and for how long it had been going on, Leena never discovered.

Be that as it may. Renate greatly enjoyed her visits and talked about a daughter, Joanna, that Edith must have had late in life and about a world-famous cellist whose name Leena knew from Classic FM. The cellist often seemed to be present during Renate's visits. In what capacity – son, nephew, Joanna's partner – Renate didn't say.

All this was happening on the periphery of Leena's life. Tom had passed away, Allan and family had moved to the Cayman Islands, where Leena visited them twice. Subsequently they moved to Berlin where she also visited them. John had been diagnosed with terminal lung cancer, so there were extra visits to Norway. Sam had returned after two years in Budapest. She was doing a lot of work for the choir, plus her own writing. In short, there was a lot going on.

Nevertheless, she enjoyed hearing about Renate's visits to St John's Wood – a breath from a world she would have loved to belong to.

Some years ago, Edith had written a book. It had been published in German and in Spanish translation. Now her greatest wish was to see it published in English. Renate and the cellist's sister, Rachel, decided to translate the book between them, with Rachel doing the bulk of the work. With Edith well into her 90s, time was not on their side, so they got on with the job as quickly as they could. Then there was the question of finding a publisher. Leena gave them the address of her own publisher, *a Sys Publishing*. She also gave Renate one of her own books to show Joanna the quality of the publishing work. The idea was to present Edith with the published translation as a surprise present for her 94th birthday. Joanna was happy and so Edith's book, *The False Houses,* was published. Renate was pleased with the finished product. According to her, the book, a series of short stories, many of them based on episodes in Edith's fascinating life, was certainly worth reading. Renate gave Leena a copy soon after it was published, which alas, Leena never got down to reading. *The False Houses* found its place under the coffee table with other unread and half-read books that Leena intended to come back to one day.

When Renate passed away, Leena was struck by guilt. She should have read the book when she was given it. Renate never said anything, but very likely she had expected Leena to read it right away and say something positive about her translation. Only when Renate was dead and buried, was the book retrieved from under the coffee table. Leena started reading and was captivated, like finding a friend where she least expected it. Some stories described episodes from what must have been Edith's teaching career, going all over London giving individual German lessons. While her sons were growing up and Leena needed her work to be flexible, she too had been going around London giving lessons, in Norwegian. The fourth story, *Finchley Road and the Swimming Pool* particularly struck a chord with her. It describes a journey on the 82 bus from Edith's home in St John's Wood to the terminus in North Finchley, a route Leena had travelled innumerable times when living in North Finchley. On the way to the swimming pool Edith is reflecting over landmarks that Leena knew well. She mentions Golders Green Crematorium where a host of celebrities are buried. People like TS Eliot, Alexander Fleming, Sigmund Freud, Rudyard Kipling, Vivian Leigh, the ballerina Anna Pavlova, Peter Sellers, George Bernard Shaw, H.G. Wells, who incidentally was born in Bromley, not far from where Leena lives. Being artistic, he must have felt drawn to North London. And that's just it. North London has long been a magnet for Jewish people and artists and intellectuals alike. And Leena, having grown up in a country where being different was frowned upon, loved it. South London has simply not attracted the same type of people.

Edith sits on the bus, reflecting about this and that, exactly the way Leena likes to do. She describes a meadow with horses and sheep and asks herself why there is such a piece of land in the middle of town. Leena remembers the farm well – a place school children were taken on outings to see live animals. Edith talks about things she sees on her way from the bus terminal to the pool, like the Pakistani news agent she used to visit with her little daughter, still there many years later. Something makes her think of a beautiful copy from 1840 of Dickens' *Pickwick Papers* that she bought in Paris. The cover was made of fine dark green leather, with gold writing. The description reminds Leena of a special edition of Bram Stoker's *Dracula* she bought in the English bookshop in Kastanjen Allee in Berlin. The book was new, and had a pale-blue and gold cover with a drawing of the Count in a black cloak with red lining. Leena knew the story, but only got down to reading it after buying the beautiful copy. In the end Edith reaches the open-air swimming pool, the very same pool where Leena and Gail used to take the children on sunny days. This was on a Sunday. Edith returned to the pool the following Saturday, but her swim was cut short. She couldn't understand why all of a sudden people got out of the water and when she followed suit and asked what was going on, she got angry looks. It turned out that a young man had just drowned, and was still in the water when Edith got in. This led to the closing of the pool and subsequently it was demolished.

The pool was closed in 1992. Before that Edith had been going there for a number of years. Leena and Tom lived in North Finchley, at three different addresses, from 1973 till 1988. So, Leena and Edith might well have been at the pool at the same time, or perhaps passed each other in the street.

*

Life is strange. You never know where fate might take you. A place you never heard of becomes your home, and a face casually observed on the Tube or in a café one day becomes your friend, as happened with Renate.

Having finished *The False Houses* Leena deeply regretted not having read it while Renate was alive. Renate had put a lot of work into it, and Leena had ignored it. Then again, who would have thought that Renate would be gone before the end of the year? Also, she wanted Edith to know how much she had enjoyed her book. But how? Renate was the only link and she was no longer there. Leena had spoken briefly to Edith's daughter at the funeral, but only enough to work out who she was. Still, with modern technology you can find somebody's address if you really put your mind to it, and one day Leena was proud to track down the daughter's e-mail address. She wrote to her, telling her about her connection with Renate, how she had been instrumental in finding a publisher for her mother's book and that she wanted Edith to know how much she had enjoyed it.

*

There are people who possess such richness of spirit that they light up the circle around them. Like attracts like, and you seldom find them among the beige anoraks of certain

101

suburbs. If by some quirk of fate, they should happen to land in such a place, they will soon find the means to get away. So, what for Renate had started as an act of charity soon became a source of enrichment and light. One of the things Renate and Leena had in common was the idea that they should have done better than living around the South-East London suburbs. Hampstead or Highgate would have suited them better, but they had never had the means to afford a house there. Small wonder then, that Renate so enjoyed her visits to St John's Wood with the vibrant old lady and the circle around her.

In 1969 Leena was living in Norway, with no plans at all to live in England. She was a serious young woman who preferred classical music to pop. Yet, she did have a few pop favourites, and the Beatles were one of them. When their album, *Abbey Road*, was released, she liked it enough to go out and buy it. Never had she imagined that way into the future, in a much-changed world, she would have reason to visit a person living next to the zebra crossing on the cover.

St John's Wood – a world of massive blocks where a small flat has the same price-tag as a house and garden in suburbia. Joanna had invited her, saying she was welcome any time after 5pm, and explained how to get there. So, on a dark Wednesday evening, here she was, armed with a bunch of pink peonies, on her way to visit Edith in her flat opposite the iconic crossing. It was the biggest block Leena had ever set foot in, and it had two entrances, one of them from Abbey Road. It wasn't easy to find, so Joanna met her in the street. They walked down two long corridors, and there it was, Edith's flat, and Edith in her hospital bed. Smiling, clearly recognisable from the photograph on the cover of her book which must have been taken at least twenty years previously. Leena particularly noticed her eyes which were the most astonishing green and surprisingly clear. Her salt and pepper hair was thick and shiny, her face radiating personality and erstwhile beauty.

It was an inspiring visit. Joanna, an attractive woman who looked too young to have a mother in her 90s, turned out to be an opera singer and an accomplished person in her own right. She disappeared into a small kitchen and returned with tea and madeleines plus strawberries and raspberries. Edith chatted away, her legs may no longer have been able to serve her, but there certainly was nothing wrong with her mind. Although she did wonder what had happened to Renate. Leena simply told her that she had died. Edith remarked that all the people she had known had passed away, and that at the age of 96, she was the only one left. From there she went on to say that because of having spent her childhood and youth in Buenos Aires, she considered herself a Latino person. As a student her group had been enjoying lectures by the great Jorge Luis Borges. He used to say, "I don't see so well". He never admitted that he didn't see at all. He lived close to the university and after the lecture, he would ask one of the students to escort him to his block of flats. One day this duty fell on Edith, and she accompanied him to his house. He told her that a good short story should either have a surprise ending, or the ending should explain its title. A treasured memory that she is still thinking about. Many years later, and after returning to Europe, she was one of the first to translate many South American writers, among them Borges, into German. A giant personality who had shone his light onto his students, and now a remnant of the very same light fell on a girl from the Norwegian forests.

As Leena was getting ready to leave, they gave her a copy of the German original of Edith's book, which Leena has been dipping in and out of. Mother and daughter both told her to visit them again. Leena replied that she would, and meant it. She was due to go to Berlin in a few days' time, but she would definitely be back upon her return. On her way to the Tube station, she stopped at the famous zebra crossing and took a few pictures, which, in the meagre light of a street lamp, came out surprisingly well.

Things don't always go as planned. Looking at her diary and the photos, she sees that the visit took place on January 22nd, the same week as she met up with Gail at British Museum and Sam went to Sarajevo. In other words, during what Leena now thinks of as the last days, when the world as we knew it was still intact. They had heard about a new virus that had sprung up in China, but nobody thought it would be more serious than SARS or bird flu, which had been a reality for a while, only to fade away, never to be heard of again. By the time she returned from Berlin, things had changed and Covid-19 was increasingly rearing its ugly head.

For this reason, Leena wasn't sure whether a visit to a person in extreme old age would be a good idea, so she never went back. And now it is too late. Weakened by two bouts of illness that may or may not have been Covid-19, she never had a test, Edith passed away on May 25th, 2020. She is now resting in the cemetery of Golders Green Crematorium, the landmark she had so often passed on the 82 bus.

Book

Two

萬物皆有其美
唯慧眼能識之

Everything has beauty, but not everyone sees it.
Confucius

Wuhan Sept 10th, 2009

Wuhan, a city few people had heard about until January 2020 when it suddenly appeared on the news as a deadly virus was spreading from its wet-market. Leena had never heard the term wet-market before, and didn't know that it is a market where they sell raw fish and meat. They sometimes also sell live wild animals, or just their meat, as with the poor pangolin, a threatened species because of its highly praised shells and meat. In China its meat is considered a delicacy and its unusual shells are used in Chinese medicine, said to have a curative effect on skin diseases and wounds. According to the organisation *Wild Aid,* the pangolin is the most trafficked and sought-after wild animal in the world. An estimated 2.7 million pangolins are hunted every year to provide scales, blood, and foetuses for the creation of various traditional Chinese medicines**.** Illegally imported pangolins from Malaysia are said to be carriers of a coronavirus that can infect humans.

With huge sums involved, there seems to be no way of stopping this cruel and scandalous trade of animals and animal parts like sea horses, musk deer glands, dried tiger penises, black bear bile and rhinoceros' horns, to mention a few, driving some species to the brink of extinction.

Apparently around two thirds of the world's infectious diseases originate from animals, especially the most feared viral diseases. For example:

Bird flu from hens.

SARS via bats and viverrids, a medium sized wolverine-like animal found mainly in South-East Asia.

MERS via bats and dromedaries.

Ebola via bats and chimpanzees.

HIV from chimpanzees.

Corona most likely via bats and pangolins.

Animals can carry the virus without themselves getting ill.

These viruses, seem to occur more frequently these days, not only due to trafficking of wild animals, but also because humans have taken over ever more of their habitats, bringing them into too close proximity with people. As a consequence, the animals no longer have the forests and jungles in which to hide. They are found ever closer to human habitation, and some of their viruses will make the jump over to humans, called spill-over. This is partly because we take over areas where animals used to live and eat the animals, and partly because they have come to live too close to us. There is little doubt that there is a connection between wild animals and corona.

Humans totally dominate the earth. The world's animal population has been more than halved in the course of the last 44 years, according to the World Wide Fund's *Living Planet report.* Today humans and their domesticated animals comprise 96% of the world's mammal population. Wild mammals comprise 4%. Man is but one of millions of species on earth, but we dominate it completely. Researchers call the times we live in *antropocen – the age of man.*

There is also the theory that this particular coronavirus originated in a research facility in Wuhan. Not far from the infamous market there are laboratories where research into coronaviruses is being carried out. Whatever the origin of the virus, out of the first 47 people infected, 27 had been visiting the market in Wuhan.

Changed animal behaviour due to the virus

Animals have started taking advantage of cities as they enter lockdown during the coronavirus pandemic. From Buenos Aires to New Delhi groups of animals including deer and lemurs have started to come out to explore – in search of food or just to play.

March 17. *A sea bird swims across clearer waters in a Venice canal.*

March 19. *A deer walks across a pedestrian crossing in Nara, Japan.*

April 4. *A herd of fallow deer graze on the lawns in front of a housing estate in Harrow Hill, East London.*

***April 8.** A herd of buffalo walk along an empty highway in New Delhi, India.*

April 10. *People jog near a jackal in Hayarcon Park in Tel Aviv, Israel. This timid animal has come into the open, reaching areas they rarely venture to as they search for food.*

April 16. *A sea lion is seen on a sidewalk of Mar del Plate harbour south of Buenos Aires, Argentina. A racoon walks in an almost deserted Central Park in New York.*

111

April 21. In Thailand and Florida leatherback sea turtles are doing better than they have done for years due to people staying off beaches.

The list goes on.

Adverse effects on animals and humans

Smog free skies and lions and hyenas strutting across fairways could easily lead us to believe that nature is thriving during the coronavirus pandemic. For some species, lockdown may indeed be good news.

In many countries, however, there has been a spike in poaching during lockdown. As well as being bad for wildlife, this raises our risk of exposure to new viruses. In the cities of rich countries, it means less traffic on the roads and less pollution, which can give wildlife space to thrive. But in rural parts of poor countries, it means some people are being driven to support themselves through poaching. Consequently, we are seeing a detrimental impact on nature because millions of people are suddenly unemployed and they have nothing to fall back on. In places like South-East Asia, there is a huge urban-to-rural migration where people have lost their jobs in the cities overnight. So, millions of people flee the cities to scrape out a living in the countryside where they have to depend on poaching, logging or other activities that are degrading nature, because they have no other option.

*

Who would have thought that a pandemic shaking the world to its foundations was to originate in a little-known city deep in China? A city Leena and Tom nearly came to visit in the early autumn of 2009. This was during what Leena calls their *travelling years*. The boys had grown up and were off their hands. Tom had taken early retirement with a good pension, and Leena was in full-time employment. So, after years of counting pennies, they found themselves affluent enough to travel to some of the world's most remote and spectacular places. Their nearly-visit to Wuhan was during a journey through China including a Yangtse river cruise, culminating in four unforgettable days in Tibet. They were part of a group consisting of Australians and Brits in more or less equal numbers. Leena does not believe in national stereotypes. All the same she is fascinated when she sees people behaving exactly according to stereotypes, as happened on this, their second Chinese journey. Their first visit was in 2006 when they followed the Silk Road from Beijing to Kashgar in Western China, close to the Pakistani border, as part of a British group, and where they saw dried-up animals for use in traditional medicine with their own eyes.

Now follow two excerpts from Leena's journals from her two voyages. Partly scribbled on a coach or a plane, and partly at night in a hotel room, when she was really too tired to write anything. At least the main experiences of the day were put down on paper before being eclipsed by the next day's adventures and events.

*

Mid-morning. Landed at Wuhan Airport. Met by male guide, young, round face, introduced himself as Jack, said they'd never be able to pronounce his Chinese name and that you couldn't find a shorter name than Jack. That set off the Australians: "Yes you can; Jim, Tim, Joe...what's shorter than Joe?" They couldn't think of anything so the game fizzled out.

The bus started. Jack did his intro about Wuhan: Capital of Hubei province, 11 million people. Lots of industry. 500 universities. Very prominent in technology and *metal urge*. Somebody suggested he might mean metallurgy. Lately lots of foreign visitors...His English left a lot to be desired; he often had 2-3 goes at a word before getting it reasonably right and then he'd laugh a short sharp laugh. He finished his speech by saying that he hoped they would be back in Wuhan to invest in its many industries and *metal urges* and that's enough for now ha-ha-ha.

No sight of the modern blocks signalling the outskirts of a major Chinese city – massive faceless blocks, perhaps 20 stories high, where people live crammed together in tiny flats. As the countryside around them deepened they realised that they would never set eyes on Wuhan and its *metal urges*.

*

Travelling at speed through a flat landscape. Everywhere water, had to be manmade, square ponds of various sizes with a strange device in the middle. In other places they saw ponds of Lotus flowers, only a few of them in bloom, some white and some bright pink, large water lilies really. At one point, gigantic bridges in the distance, a lofty spaghetti junction, almost lace-like, graceful and elegant. Part of the much talked about economic miracle that has not trickled down to the poorer parts of the population. Leena expected Jack to say something about the junction, but no.

Earlier on, when finishing his recital, Jack had asked if anyone had any questions, presumably about the industries and *metal urges* of Wuhan. He belonged to the type of guide they had seen on their previous visit to China. Having never set foot outside their country, they have little idea of what seems exotic and interesting to a Westerner. Also, having been fed communist propaganda from an early age they are proud to show off their country's material accomplishments. And of course, Big Brother might be watching so they'd better be careful about what they say.

Australian Margaret wanted to know about all the square ponds.

"Fish farms."

"And the device in the middle?"

"For oxygen." End of story.

Somebody else wanted to know about the gigantic lily-pads.

"Lotus plants." Leena could have told them that. "People cultivate lotus plants because many people like to eat the roots, for example my daughter, ha-ha-ha." Then silence. Leena would have liked to know something about the spaghetti junction but couldn't be bothered to ask. She drifted off to sleep, then woke up to look at the land-scape. Completely flat, green, poplars – otherworldly, like something out of an ancient painting. At one stage flow-ers along the road, perhaps orange and red marigolds plus some sort of yellow lilies. Here and there a canal stretching out into a misty horizon. Charcoal-grey buffaloes grazing by the waterside. Also a few white ibis-birds with them. Another canal disappearing into the mist. People working the land in cone-shaped hats. Here and there an old man tending a buffalo. Road completely straight. At intervals large boards with writing in Chinese and English: NO TIREDNING WHEN DRIVING. NO DRINKING DRIVING, etc. They stopped outside a service station for people to go to the loo. Two tiny old women walk-ing about with sacks, happy wrinkly faces, near toothless gums. They understood that they were meant to put any rubbish they might have in their sacks.

And so, the day continued. At one stage the Australians started singing to alleviate the boredom, but they soon ran out of steam. Leena was not bored. After all, how often do you get to travel through the deep Chinese countryside? Leena loves travelling, has done ever since her first journey outside Norway at the age of eight, travelling through southern Sweden, eyes glued to the landscape looking for windmills and anything else that seemed strange and different. But here, most of her travel companions were bored.

They stopped for a meal in a town whose name Leena failed to register, too late for lunch and too early for dinner, but a good meal all the same. Lots of different Chinese delicacies. Leena has developed a liking for steamed buns – white, and completely tasteless, yet surprisingly satisfying.

Soon darkness was falling and Jack told them that they were approaching the place where they would be boarding the boat for their Yangtze cruise.

They turned off the main road, driving slowly through what looked like slums; the worst hovels Leena had ever seen. Dark and dingy holes in the cliff walls, allowing a glimpse of a crude wooden table and chairs. In some of these dwellings people were selling sweets and soft drinks. Outside one such home a family group was doing exercises to a TV-programme.

Finally, off the coach. Very uneven road or rather footpath. A faint street lamp here and there, far from enough to illuminate the treacherous surface full of deep holes and cracks. One unlucky step and you could easily end up with a broken ankle. Pitch dark, humid and slightly misty. Somebody, probably Jack, walking in front shining a torch behind him so they could watch their step. Between the trees Leena caught her first glimpse of the mighty Yangtze River, a shimmering, gleaming golden surface in the dark. The frogs in the bushes were laying on a tremendous concert to welcome them. She really wanted to enjoy their chorus but it was difficult because the Australians found the dodgy surface so hilarious that they couldn't stop shrieking and laughing, totally drowning out the frogs.

Kashgar Market, September 2006

All day on the move. Coach to the animal market. Farmers from the surrounding areas bring in animals they want to sell on lorries and donkey carts. Sheep stowed on top of each other worse than people in the London Underground. Impossible to see where one animal finished and another one started. People this far west no longer look Chinese, they are Uyghurs – Turkish-Afghan looking people, and Muslims. Their music, blaring out here and there, is indistinguishable from Arabic music, at least to Western ears. Finding herself in this alien environment brought home to Leena how the Muslim world stretches on and on, from Morocco to way inside China. Most of the people in the market were men – Afghan faces, scruffy not very clean clothes, most of them in Islamic box hats and long dark coats. Stalls selling strange hot food, no idea what it might be. Lots of dust and dirt. Never occurred to a townie like Leena that an animal market in the desert would have to be very dusty. Lorries driving through generating clouds of fine sand. Animals seemed very docile. A tiny calf was tethered next to some fully grown cows. It let out the saddest little *moo*. They trudged along for quite some time, their local guide, Camille, leading the way, sun beating down, dust settling in their hair. Camille, told them that right now a part of Kashgar was closed to tourists because they were filming *The Kite Runner*. Based on a gripping novel set in Afghanistan by the Afghan-American writer Khaled Hosseini. As Afghanistan was out of bounds, this was the place that most resembled it. Leena has read the book and seen the film.

On to the famous Kashgar bazaar, supposedly the biggest Sunday market in the world. It is not out in the desert surrounded by camels the way Leena had imagined, but covered and inside the town. Dave, their tour leader, took them to some sort of a shop in the centre where there was tea brewing and paper cups so they could help themselves, plus two sofas to sit and rest on.

And so, they sauntered around. A town within the town. Not really crowded, a mixture of locals and Western tourists. Avenue upon avenue of stalls. Some with strange fruit heaped high, others with ingredients for Chinese medicine. They saw eggs where tiny dead foetuses could be seen through holes in the shells. Piles of dried up snakes and lizards, heaps of dried animal bits and ground-up powders in many colours whose origins nobody could guess, like a witches' shopping mall. In other avenues rows of furs. There was one avenue where they sold nothing but shoes, and another filled with kitchen utensils, on and on. At first Tom and Leena were walking with little Margaret, one of their travel companions who was over 80, although nobody would have given her a day over 70. Her friend, Lizzie, was tired and wanted to rest on one of the sofas. Yesterday, on a daytrip high in the Karakoram mountains, the altitude had got to her and she nearly fainted. This morning Leena heard Dave telling her that she looked better. She replied, "It won't last, dear, this is killing me." She's a tall, thin 73-year-old, with manor house written all over her. The schedule of constantly being on the go is more than she bargained for. After a while, Margaret wanted to return to Lizzie. Tom and Leena were disorientated and needed to focus to find their way back. But Margaret remembered. Never had they seen an 83-year-old like her! Lizzie was fast asleep when they returned. Having deposited Margaret and had a rest and a cup of tea, they wandered off again. This time they came across a section where the stalls were piled high with roll upon roll of red, green, yellow, blue and flowery silk, all with sequins and beads – material for the type of dresses that local women were wearing. Seeing all the women in dresses fit for Buckingham Palace, Leena assumed they were on their way to some celebration or other. But Camille said no, these are the type of dresses they like to wear. She bought some saffron and two translucent white stone eggs that looked like they had a light in the centre.

*

And now? Will she go on a major journey ever again? Probably not. If the world gets back to some kind of normality, it is unlikely to be as we knew it. One budget airline reckons it will take two years before air travel gets back to pre-corona levels. And do we really want it to return to what it was? Leena is painfully aware that people like her, with their passion for jetting off to far-away places, had caused the virus to spread like wild-fire across the world. This summer, apart from the usual trips to Norway and Berlin, she had planned to visit Transylvania – the deep dark forests with their tales of vampires and werewolves had always held a fascination to her. She had been hoping to go to Tierra del Fuego, Land of Fire, on the southern tip of Argentina. Coming from the North, she would love to see the extreme South with its stunning glaciers. With less air pollution, perhaps the climate change might slow down, and the ice stop melting at the present alarming rate, until the powers that be finally see sense and do something to stop it.

April 20th, 2020

Attention in Whitehall has turned to fleshing out an exit strategy from the lockdown to fire up the economy. Scientists are advising Downing Street against relaxing the lockdown prematurely.

As the lockdown nears the three-week mark, people want to know when the restrictions will be lifted. But it also matters how *they are lifted.*

Nobody should kid themselves that this can be purely a technical matter left to scientists, doctors and economists. Lives and livelihoods are at stake. Deciding the best course of action will involve grappling with massive ethical issues.

How much of an economic hit should we take to save lives? To what extent should we sacrifice the livelihoods of the young to protect the old? Should the vulnerable be locked up against their will?

There is talk of young people having their careers disrupted, how having to stay home robs them of the chance to go out and find a partner . . . But what about the young during the first and second world wars who had their lives disrupted for years, and millions of them perished along the way? Did they whinge about having their careers and lives put on hold? To them it was clear cut. They were fighting a war with a visible enemy and the enemy had to be vanquished before any kind of normality could be restored. The young have time on their side. What's a couple of years in the scheme of an 80-year-long lifetime? We too are fighting an enemy, but the way to victory does not lead through guns and bomber planes. All we need is to stop the virus from spreading by keeping to ourselves. Unfortunately, often easier said than done. Not everybody can work from home, and not everybody has spacious homes where they can isolate. Naturally, if a doctor has to choose between saving a 70-year-old and a 20-year-old, the choice should be clear-cut. But what if the 20-year-old is a criminal waster heading for a life behind bars, and the 70-year-old is fit and healthy and fulfilling a valuable role in society? Not so clear-cut then is it? Then again … the 20-year-old might mend his ways, and the 70-year-old might have an undiagnosed disease that will claim her life in a year's time. Humans should not be asked to play God.

Easter has been and gone. Another weekend is over.

Monday morning. The magnolia tree outside her window has shed most of its blooms. Pink petals scattered on the grass, but there are still some flowers left. Its leaves are already big. The sky is luminous and nearly white. No cloud to be seen. Once again, a blanket of tiny ice crystals hangs between heaven and earth. With no large jets polluting the atmosphere and fewer cars on the roads, the air is crystalline and clear. More birds are singing than in recent years. There appears to be more insects as well. With humans, the scourge of the planet, lying low – is nature already making a come-back? Wouldn't it be wonderful if it was? With a visible improvement, perhaps even the sceptics, who doggedly refuse to believe in climate change, might accept that scientists and environmentalists have a point.

Sceptics, "There have always been temperature fluctuations."

"Yes, true, but isn't it too much of a coincidence that rising temperatures happen to coincide with an unequalled rise in pollution?"

Sceptics, "There have always been temperature fluctuations.

"Perhaps we are in a period of naturally rising temperatures, but one does not exclude the other. It would do no harm to reduce the emissions of greenhouse gases."

Sceptics, "There have always been temperature fluctuations."

But what if rain started to fall on land that has been parched for years? What if the parts of the earth with dying crops suddenly came back to life? Would they believe then? Things are changing. Toxic megacities like Bangkok, Beijing, São Paolo and Bogotá, where coronavirus restrictions have been imposed, all report an unprecedented decline in pollution. With the streets being empty of cars and the air empty of planes, cities can see blue skies. Suddenly mountains and landmarks that for years have been disappearing in a mist of pollution are seen clearly. In Pathankot, in the Punjab, the snow-covered Himalayas can be seen for the first time in 30 years. Cali, Colombia's usually smoky and congested metropolis, has been spared the usual forest fires, as the thick cloud that normally hangs over the city has been lifted. In France, the Eiffel Tower is again seen clearly from the Parisian suburb of Saint Cloud.

However, there is a cruel irony: with most residents of these cities strictly confined to their homes, few are able to appreciate this newly fresh air, except through an open window or from their balconies.

It is estimated that over the months of coronavirus lockdown there have been some 11,000 fewer deaths from air pollution in the UK and elsewhere in Europe.

Murky seas around Britain are transformed into crystal-clear Caribbean-style waters thanks to lower pollution. Places like The Isle of Wight and Portsmouth are again enjoying clean blue waters along their shores. With lockdown forcing humans to stay away from the sea, noise pollution is virtually gone.

For millions of years land and sea animals lived in well-defined worlds. A new two-legged species did make it out onto the water, but their vessels were small and quiet and rarely ventured far from land. Then steamships were invented. They were noisy and criss-crossed the oceans like never before. The whales did not like it at all. With their special language made up of clicks and what to human ears sounds like song, they had always been able to communicate across vast distances of ocean. Gradually the ships grew in numbers and were made bigger and noisier, drowning out the songs of the whales, confusing them and ruining their communication. So, there they were, making their way through noisy and murky waters, wondering what had happened to their world. But now, with most large ships lying idle, they are again communicating and their songs can be herd where no whale-song has been herd for countless years, as once again they frolic in the crystalline waters of the endless sea.

Unfortunately, we might only be seeing a temporary respite. The powers that be are desperate to get the economy going again, and with it the pollution that's killing the planet. Will our so-called leaders take on board what happened to the environment during lockdown and reduce the consumption of fossil fuels? Perhaps, but not enough to make a real difference. Or, will they continue to laugh in the faces of people who care? Very likely.

*

The weekend was dead. Nancy le Fort has decided to do online choir practice even though the planned summer concert on July 4th is highly unlikely to take place. She wants to get them singing again. More than anything else it's an initiative to break the monotony of lockdown, and to keep the choir ticking over until better times, whenever that might be. She has set up virtual meetings on an application called Zoom. Apparently, it has been in common use for a while and some choir members were already on Zoom for activities like pilates and yoga. But Leena had never heard of it. In the old world, she would have asked Allan or Sam to set it up for her. In the new world, she has no option but to do it herself. She couldn't believe it when she'd actually got it to work. They met for a 40 minutes' session at 11am on Saturday. It was lovely to see Nancy and choir members again, although only about half of them had made it onto Zoom.

Later in the day she'd had a FaceTime session with Amelia, who hasn't forgotten her and still wants to talk to Nanny. The little girl loves reading to her, and to hear Leena telling her one of the stories that she invents on the spot, and then promptly forgets, but now she is running out of ideas.

That was Saturday, which had its bright moments, but was dreary all the same. On Sunday morning Allan rang her from his office to discuss business with her. With the two little girls at home all the time, he and Elida have to grab time for work when they can. At the age of 44 he has begun to trust Leena's judgement, although she was never a business person, a portion of good common sense can solve many a problem. Amelia tried to get through to her while she was talking to Allan and texted her a lot of stickers. Later on, a bite of lunch on the decking, which is shielded from the wind on two sides. The sun felt beautiful and warm. The ground is extremely dry and cracks are beginning to appear. Leena spent a long time watering her rose bushes. Then she decided to take her daily walk. Out in the open the wind was cold and blustery, almost hostile, like the ogre next door who was outside, scraping moss from between the bricks on his patio. Seeing Leena, he straightened, as though wanting to speak to her. Leena pretended not to notice. Very likely he would blame the moss on her trees again: trees drop leaves and attract birds and insects, messing up his garden, producing moss and weeds that he has to spend hours to get rid of. She gets away, before he says anything. The wind really is cold. She decides to return to the house and put on a jacket before starting her walk. But then Nina rings her from Norway on her landline to offer the latest in the puppy saga. She'd bought a cute Pomeranian puppy called Matheo, who turns out to be too much of a handful, exhausting Timo, who at the ripe old age of 13, prefers to spend his life sleeping. He's exhausting Nina as well, constantly running around and needing to go out for a wee ten times a day starting at 5 in the morning. Sometimes he wees on the floor. Nina spoke at great length about how and why she had decided to sell the puppy because it was all too much.

By the end of the conversation, Leena felt exasperated and had lost the will to go walking. The rest of the day drifted by with social media, washing her hair and cooking a stir-fry for dinner. Sam rang telling her that he had made chicken stock from the carcass of the roast chicken he and his housemate had had for dinner yesterday. He had never done anything like that before. Lockdown is definitely having an effect on people, making them test out new recipes and skills, like her friend, Clare, a keen sports woman who has taken to knitting toy animals. She's good at it, too.

April 21st, 2020

Today the sky is a pure light blue, but only 11 degrees. The magnolia tree is moving in a strong breeze, no doubt making it feel colder than it really is. These beautiful sunny days have a sting in their tail in more ways than one. Whether the icy wind is our Lord's way to encourage people to stay home, or to laugh in their faces, is hard to decide. Could be a bit of both, but the wind definitely feels hostile.

Sam rang last night as he always does. After some chit-chat, he said, "You don't need to worry about me and coronavirus any more, because I've had it."

"What do you mean, had it?"

"I've had it. I was ill for a week."

"When was that?"

"Last week, I didn't tell you because I didn't want to worry you."

"So, when you were talking to me, pretending that everything was all right and you were out walking, you were actually ill in bed with coronavirus. How can I know you are telling the truth now, that you are not still ill or even in hospital?"

It transpired that he had started to feel bad on Easter Monday. During the night he'd had a lot of strange, vivid dreams. That must have been the day he told Leena that he was feeling upset because he had been dreaming about his father. The sudden loss had affected him badly. From a family of six, Tom, Leena, Sam, Allan, Elida and Amelia, there were only Leena and Sam left in London. With Tom gone, and Allan and his family having moved away, first to the Cayman Islands and then to Berlin, life could feel empty. Allan has his life to live and his stories to write, she understands that. Besides, having abandoned her own parents in the same way, she is not in a position to complain. All the same, she can't help wishing that things had been different.

Be that as it may. After a disturbed night, Sam developed a high temperature and a headache, plus a complete loss of appetite. His food tasted of nothing, which is another symptom. However, he did not have a cough, which meant that his lungs had not been attacked. He spent most of the week in bed. His housemate, Nick, was a great support, and did not get ill. One friend, a Mexican called Alberto, now living in Vienna with his girlfriend, texted him every day to see how he was. Upon being told about his illness, another so-called friend did not contact him once.

While all this was going on, Leena had been living in sweet ignorance, thinking that all was well. Sam was right, she would have been worried out of her mind if she'd known. On the other hand, it highlights the limitations of phone calls and online communication. You hear their voices and see their words on a screen, but you have no way of knowing whether a person is out for a stroll or lying in his sickbed. Sam doesn't use FaceTime, which would have let the cat out of the bag. Allan communicates via FaceTime and sends a lot of photos, so she can see that he and his family are all well and active, a blessing if ever there was one.

Sam said that one of Nick's friends had had the coronavirus quite badly. He was coughing up blood, which meant that his lungs had been attacked. His girlfriend who'd been looking after him, had not been ill at all. However, chances are that she has still caught the virus and that she might be a carrier. Neither Sam nor Nick's friend contacted a doctor. That's two cases of people being infected without reporting it. No doubt there are thousands, if not millions of similar cases up and down the country. This means that the number of infections by far exceeds the official figures.

So, Sam took ill on Easter Monday. What was Leena doing on that day? She remembers what she did on Easter Sunday. It was a bright and sunny day and she walked all the way to the cemetery to visit Tom's grave – a dreary walk through faceless suburban streets – no children out playing, no life except for a few people walking their dogs or hurrying to or from their cars. And, when she got there, the gate was locked. Normally she would take the tram or a bus part of the way, but these days she prefers to shun public transport. On her way back, she ran into Patsy and Mike out on their daily walk. Patsy is the same age as Leena, Mike a year younger. Two more people who are not heeding the government's instruction to stay home. She hadn't seen them for weeks. With everybody in lockdown, the only time you see people is if you happen to meet them in the street. They stopped and had a chat, on the pavement, six metres apart. The only people she'd talked to all day. Be careful what you wish for, it may come true. Leena can't help thinking of her breaks in

Norway when she wanted to be alone, and felt thwarted when well-meaning relations turned up to keep her company. She's got enough time to herself now.

Easter Monday? What was she doing then? She can't remember. Probably writing her journal, online communication and social media. A bit of gardening, a walk, cooking, watching TV, knitting... That's life when one day is just like the one before and the one after – like identical beads in a necklace. Impossible to tell them apart. And on that dreary day, Sam was taken seriously ill, and she knew nothing about it. Or was it the day the ogre had accosted her from across the fence? Yes, that must have been the day. She was on her way out, but then she heard, "Hm, eh-hm, have you got a moment?" And there he was, too close for comfort, a wizened old man dressed in a threadbare suit, shorter than Leena, and she is 5' 5", his piercing little eyes boring into her:

"When are you going to cut down your eucalyptus tree then?"

"I'm not."

"Its roots are reaching right into my garden."

"The roots would still be there even if the tree was cut down."

"Yes, but they wouldn't be sucking up moisture from my lawn if the tree was dead, would they? I want it chopped down."

In order to get away, Leena said she would think about it. The wrong thing to say of course. He would take it to mean that she would have it done.

131

*

In hindsight, having had time to absorb the shock, Leena is grateful that Sam had not told her about having the virus until he was on the mend, and that he had only had it mildly.

September 14th, 2009

White mountain peaks above a layer of white cloud. The Himalayas outside their window and below them. The Aussies were laughing and carrying on for a while, but now they have quietened down. Most likely they have gone to sleep. Leena can't believe her luck. She read in the guidebook that those sitting by the window on the left side are in for a real treat – passing Mount Everest. This is a large plane, two seats either side and four in the middle. Leena got a left-hand window seat. Tom next to her. Those sitting in the middle see very little. She feels almost guilty about it, but it was pure luck. They all took the seats they were allocated, and their Chinese tour leader, Lisa, checked them in as a group. Looks like they are flying south-west. Nothing but mountains as far as the eye can see, sharp, craggy, covered in snow. And there it is, Mount Everest, easily recognisable from hundreds of photographs, rising above the clouds. Leena hurries to take a picture before it disappears behind them. Tibor, the Hungarian, is stretching over them hoping to get a photo. Leena offers to move out of the way, but the people behind them have already offered to take the picture for him. Tibor and Zsofia – both Hungarians living in Australia, having escaped from communism in the 1960s. They are friendly enough, but still somewhat apart from the rest of the group, nothing you can really put your finger on, or perhaps it is because of always speaking Hungarian between themselves. Both of them are slim and young-looking, both have longish blond hair. Youthful clothes too. Only their faces tell a different story. Two youngsters on the threshold of old age. For some reason they don't appear to like Leena. When they were visiting the ancient City Wall in Xi'an, beautiful and dreamy, stretching on and on into a fine mist, all Leena wanted to do was to spend their half-hour of free time walking along it, but then Lisa said it was time to come with her to the watchtower to see the view. Leena said to Zsofia, because she happened to be nearest, "I'm really fed up with being shunted around all the time."

Zsofia replied, "Why don't you go and sit in the bus then?"

They are coming in for landing in Lhasa. Will she be able to feel the peace and silence of the mountains? She'll have to wait and see.

Below she can see a wide river, a road, and groups of small stone houses surrounded by ranges of craggy mountains. Everything looks grey and army brownish-green. She had no idea what Tibetan houses might look like. Now they are circling just above the mountains, so close you can see the details. Then a flat stretch of land with sandbanks and green water—a river estuary, the river dividing up then joining together again. Sand, green water and a few bushes surrounded by endless rugged mountains.

Some places are hell and some are heaven. Cairo, in Leena's opinion, is hell – the noise, the pollution, the crowds … Tibet is heaven. Air so wonderfully clean and fresh. Sharp-edged mountains silhouetted against a crisp blue sky. Nice and warm. Their local guide is a young woman called Diki. Very kind sincere face.

Seen on the way from the airport: calves in a street, first two, then two more. She doesn't know if they are cows or yaks. Lots of prayer flags hanging along the river. In one place the river runs very white – prayer flags suspended above it. Quite a lot of cows or yaks. The river is called Lhasa River. Diki says people don't eat the fish in the river because it is holy. Also because of the dead people in it. Later Leena asked her what she meant. She replied that when people die, they get cut up and chucked in the river to feed the fish. The body-parts are wrapped in a white scarf. She said special people up in the mountain perform the task. Leena would have thought people would want to eat the fish to complete the circle, but evidently not. There is a ceremony before the body is carried up into the mountains. In his book, *To a Mountain in Tibet*, Colin Thubron visits one of these places and describes it as the most frighteningly bleak place you could think of.

*

Subdued atmosphere at lunch. People were tired after having to get up at 4.30am. Even the Aussies were quiet.

Time for a rest now. Leena felt very lacking in energy. Being vegetarian, the food she could eat was insubstantial, only vegetables and boiled rice. The others had meat. There was some scrambled eggs and tomatoes too, but everybody wanted some, so Leena ended up having very little. A fight almost broke out over a bottle of Pepsi. Leena doesn't normally drink Pepsi, but needing a boost, she did then. Back to their room for a rest. Leena ate a piece of chocolate and felt some energy returning. Meanwhile Tom had fallen asleep. Leena was tired. But no, she had not come to Tibet to rest in a hotel room.

Outside on her own. She was so happy. One walk down the street by herself was worth ten organised tours of the city, marched from A to B to C, crossing the street like a crocodile of schoolchildren. So, this then, was Lhasa, the capital of Tibet. One long street, shops on both sides, nothing fancy – hairdressers, one working outside combing a woman's long black hair. Leena is walking slowly – jeans, sunglasses, hat on her head, short-sleeved top – she doesn't notice anyone else in short sleeves. The street is sunny on one side, shady on the other. It's gone 4 in the afternoon. A woman in a long black native dress and apron smiles at her. Leena smiles back. Diki told them how to say hello in Tibetan, but Leena has forgotten it already. It would have been good if she'd remembered. She would so much have liked to interact with the locals, if only with a smile and a hello. On the sunny side, the mountains are quite close, on Leena's side, which is shady, further away. She would have liked to cross the streets, but it looks too treacherous. Two lines of traffic in each direction. There is a zebra crossing with a traffic light, but drivers don't appear to take it seriously. No traffic island in the middle. The traffic is not very heavy, but she would still have to take her chances. She doesn't much fancy being knocked down.

She walks on. Street hawkers sitting on the pavement – colourful necklaces, bracelets and ornaments on blankets in front of them. She walks past, doesn't react to their "looki, looki." Lots of hawkers, all selling the same things. Leena looks at her watch and decides it's time to turn back. If Tom wakes up and finds her gone, he'll be worried. A beautiful young woman – dark skin, native dress, shouts out, "Hello, looki, looki!" Leena replies OK, and points to her watch, indicating she'll be back tomorrow. The woman picks up a bracelet of royal blue beads with one large amber bead in the centre and puts it on Leena's wrist. It suits her so well. She says, "how much?" The woman takes her hand in both of hers, they are cool and soft, and says, "no, bomba." She repeats this several times. Leena thinks it means that she can pay for it tomorrow when she comes back to buy more things, but she'll ask Diki. She doesn't mind buying things from street hawkers, they have hard lives. You have to bargain, of course, but within reason. Some tourists feel so victorious if they manage to knock the price down to next to nothing. But after all, what does it matter to Leena whether she pays £1 or £1.50 for a little bracelet. It may, however, matter a lot to the hawker.

The Dalai Lama

There are three holy lakes in Tibet. When the old Dalai Lama has died, the high lamas sit by a holy lake and prey for eight days. On the eight day, an image will appear on the surface of one of the lakes. They will see a house and a woman sitting outside cradling a baby. Then the quest is to find the baby. Before the old Dalai Lama dies, he will often give some idea of where his reincarnation can be found.

After passing a series of tests to see if the infant really is the incarnation of the previous Dalai Lama, the child will be taken away from his family and never be able to return to them. But his family can come and visit him. There is a room in the Summer Palace where he can see his family, in particular his mother, but his mother is not allowed to spend the night in the palace.

*

Sun, peace, palaces and prayer wheels. The Chinese may have conquered their land, but they haven't conquered their spirit.

May 4th, 2020

Time drifts by, imperceptibly. Today it is two months to the day since March 4th when Leena got the idea to chronicle the advance of the coronavirus, and its effect on her and her family's lives. It's a Monday; next Monday will be the 11th and exactly three months since February

137

11th when she embarked on her last visit to Berlin before the virus made travel, at first unsafe, and then out of the question.

Before the 4th comes the 3rd. In her lifetime Leena has lived through a great many 3rds of May, but only two of them were special enough to stand out. It was on a May 3rd, back in the early 1970s that she arrived in Paris as a young student and was blown away by the buildings, the streets, the cafés, the markets, the people, the sounds, the blossom, the smells ... Everything so much more exciting than in poor old Norway. She felt at home right away and very soon she had taken on the mannerisms and dress sense of a French person. Has her frenchness stayed with her till this day? On the outside, perhaps; she is fastidious about the way she looks. But on the inside there remains a portion of the Nordic melancholia that she has never quite managed to shift. And why should she? Why this modern obsession with being happy all the time? Life is not like that. So why not welcome the sadness as a friend rather than an enemy that needs to be banished?

Her most memorable May 3rd, however, came nine years later, the day Sam was born, on the Saturday of May bank holiday, 1980.

So, yesterday was his 40th birthday – for many an unwelcome milestone – half your life gone, and what have you made of it? Add coronavirus, lockdown, no gatherings allowed, so no party. His brother and family out of reach in Berlin and his mother on the opposite side of London, self-isolating like everyone else. It was not a day he anticipated with joy. He was fairly sure he'd had the virus, but he couldn't be 100 per cent certain. Besides, it has not been established how much immunity it would give him. The NHS is too overstretched to test people like him for antibodies.

But then, in the morning, messages and phone calls started to arrive, even from people he hadn't seen in years. Amelia and Lea phoned him on FaceTime from Berlin with an arrangement of "Happy Birthday" that they had made especially for him. Amelia had put on a pretty dress and had a new hairstyle because she wanted everything to be perfect. After that, he met up with a good friend and they went for a walk around Walthamstow Marshes. He then made his way across London by Tube for the first time in a month. Once there he took a welcome opportunity to walk around for a while. After weeks of hardly setting foot outside Walthamstow, finding himself in central London felt positively exciting. Very few people about, totally different from the London he knew. The sight of a city void of life felt surreal. No crowds cramming the pavements. Streets empty, except for the odd bus, car or cyclist. Shops and restaurants closed, looking dark and forsaken. Leena would have found the empty streets and darkened shops and restaurants eerie, but Sam said, "No. Not eerie, just surreal." He saw more people when he ventured into St James Park and Green Park, but most of the benches were empty and so were the lawns apart from a few individuals here and there. A city is meant to be full of people, and when it isn't, it feels unnatural, almost ghostly – when you walk along and all you can hear is the sound of your own footsteps . . . Leena experienced the feeling many years ago in Oslo, at Easter, when the capital's citizens take to the mountains for skiing and sunshine on snow. Having visited her ageing auntie, who'd had nothing to offer her but coffee and biscuits, and having skipped lunch, she was starving. With half an hour's wait for her bus home, she walked around the empty streets looking for an open kiosk or snack bar where she could buy a hotdog, but found neither . . .

After Sam's visit to the parks, followed a 20 minutes' train ride from a near-deserted Victoria Station, and that was positively eerie. All the fast food outlets closed, hardly any passengers about. Everywhere notices that you should avoid the trains unless you had a good reason for travelling. Guards in psychedelic pink vests at every entrance making sure nobody got on a train without a face mask. Sam felt that he shouldn't be there. He decided that bringing food for his mother must be a valid enough reason, which was what he was going to say if questioned by the transport police. Besides, it was true, he was planning to stop at Leena's local M&S to get her some much longed-for goodies. Apart from a couple of expeditions to her Sainsbury Local down the road, Leena had not set foot inside a shop since before lockdown. She had already sent him his card and present in case things went wrong on the day, and for some reason he couldn't make it to her house. He had asked her if she could bake Norwegian waffles with strawberry jam, his childhood favourite, reminding him of happy summers with his grandmother in Norway. He had loved the house in the forest, still does. As a child and teenager, he would sit in what used to be John's room and read, then go jogging along the not-very-busy road skirting the lake. The main road between Oslo and Hønefoss runs on the opposite side of the lake. The energies of the house feel less homely now, not the same at all.

The original plan had been to deposit the shopping on the doorstep, and for them to take a walk in the park, eating their waffles whilst keeping a reasonably safe distance on a bench. But then Leena thought; what the heck? It's his birthday, what's the problem? We can open the windows and sit either end of the table, it's nearly two metres long. Sam had bought bread and brie as well, and had managed to get hold of a jar of proper Norwegian strawberry jam. Leena already had tomatoes and olives, and had made fresh blackberry jam from berries she had picked and frozen last autumn. Sam doesn't drink alcohol, so no wine or Prosecco, and he didn't mind about a cake. The waffles were enough. A long time since Leena has baked waffles, she used to do it often when the boys were young. She'd even lugged her waffle-maker to work once a year and made waffles for her students, always popular. A few years ago now, but she hadn't forgotten the art.

After the meal they left the house, both wearing a face mask, mainly in case the ogre next door should spot them coming out of the house together and report them to the police, it is the sort of thing he has been known to do in the past. However, he was nowhere to be seen. Keeping their distance, they soon took off their masks. The wide expanse of common was virtually empty, and walking with a face mask does affect your breathing. So, there they were, a simple walk first across the common and then through the park and around the lake. Back through the little wood and across the common again. A luminous evening, the wonderful light of a clear sky at sunset. What could be better? In spite of the negative circumstances, Sam said it had turned out to be one of the best birthdays he'd ever had.

And, another 3rd of May for Leena to remember.

*

On the 15th of March the Health Secretary, Matt Hancock, confirmed that people over 70 will be told to stay at home for four months to stem the spread of coronavirus. A flawed argument if ever there was one as the elderly is the group that tends to spend the least amount of time in crowded clubs and pubs and packed public transport.

Apart from a foray into central London, shortly before the ban on going out for over 70s', and a couple of visits to local shops, Leena has been keeping a low profile anyway, but to be told to more-or-less stay indoors for four months! She shudders to think what it might do to her mental and physical health. She felt singled out. There is age and there is age. She knows for sure that she is fitter than many people 10-20 years younger. It depends on your genetic makeup and lifestyle. It's foolish simply to divide the population by a crude age-based cut-off point that would condemn a large number of healthy people to months of misery and isolation. If coronavirus doesn't get them, isolation, loneliness and lack of exercise and outside stimuli will. Ridiculous, just look at all the actors, musicians and TV-presenters, still going strong into their 80s.

When these measures were first announced Leena didn't take them too personally. She knew she was healthy, and who was to stop her sneaking out for a lone walk after dark, or pop into an uncrowded shop with a face mask? Besides, she had a garden where there was always work to be done, some of it quite heavy, so good exercise there. She knew she was privileged.

Then on March 23rd came general lockdown for all. It made her feel better. Other people could go for a walk and go out for necessary shopping etc., so why not she? It blurred the edges, and most of the people of 70+ that she knew behaved like everyone else. It made her feel part of the human family again, in the same boat as everybody else. But now, with talks of easing lockdown for the general public, but not for the over 70s, she feels angry and discriminated against, singled out, no longer part of humanity. It means she couldn't have had a day like yesterday and neither could Sam. They weren't flouting the rules of lockdown, simply applying them with a bit of common sense, and so it should be. The most she could hope for under the rules of isolation, if she has understood the latest information films correctly, would be for Sam to come to the house, put the shopping on her doorstep, and "touch" hands through the window pane. How extremely sad! And she, poor useless oldy, was supposed to smile and be happy as she waved him goodbye.

She would most certainly resent a do-gooder, one year her junior, coming to her house "touching" hands through the windowpane and asking if she needed anything. Far from making her feel grateful, it would make her reach for a shotgun.

Turns out she is not the only person feeling like this. Her views are shared by a lot of people, some with enough influence to be listened to, like the actor and broadcaster Sir Michael Palin and the ageism tsar Ros Altmann. They have both joined calls for the government not to exclude healthy pensioners if lockdown restrictions are relaxed. Leading medical professionals have said that excluding any section of the population from easing of lockdown based solely on age would be discriminatory.

Meanwhile, the health secretary, Matt Hancock, tweeted: "We have strongly advised all over 70s to follow social distancing measures. However, there is no 'blanket ban', and the suggestion that the clinically vulnerable "include 'people aged 70 or older regardless of medical conditions' is wrong and deeply misleading."

This prompted some people on social media to point to government advice published on Friday May 1st, which includes the words: "Clinically vulnerable people are those aged 70 or older (regardless of medical condition ...)"

So, it appears that Leena's initial interpretation of the guidelines was not wrong at all. The right honourable gentleman has backtracked in the face of public opposition. Leena will keep up the social distancing, as should everybody. It is in people's best interest and a small price to pay compared to what goes on in hospitals up and down the country.

News of the day

The UK's coronavirus death toll has become the world's second-highest, according to data released by the Office for National Statistics, with the total passing 30,000. Biggest failure in a generation. Where did Britain go wrong?

Health Secretary Matt Hancock was midway through a radio interview when the phone call came through live to air. On the line was Intisar Chowdhury, whose father, Abdul, had made a prescient public plea to Boris Johnson in late March.

Through a Facebook post, the 53-year-old consultant urologist for a London hospital had urged the Prime Minister to make sure every health worker in Britain would be given protective equipment during the coronavirus pandemic. Abdul Mabud Chowdhury died just three weeks later, after contracting the disease.

In his phone call, the doctor's grieving son asked for answers and an apology: "The public is not expecting the government to handle this perfectly," he told Hancock. "We just want you to openly acknowledge that there have been mistakes in handling the virus, especially to me and to so many families that have lost loved ones as a result of this virus and probably as a result of the government not handling it seriously enough."

Chowdhury seemingly spoke on behalf of a growing chorus of health experts, MPs and members of the public who think Britain's response to the crisis has suffered from a series of deadly mistakes and miscalculations.

*

The government's mishandling of the crisis during the early days of the pandemic is well documented and publicised. However, the honourable gentlemen insist on brushing their mistakes under the carpet hoping nobody will notice, or be too stupid to understand.

At the beginning of the pandemic, the country's experts maintained that any steps taken to slow the spread of the disease domestically needed to be timed intelligently, to ensure that they covered the peak of the crisis. If a lockdown were ordered too early, it would suppress the disease and save lives in the short term, but only delay the inevitable outbreak, and potentially make it worse by pushing it into the winter, a time when flu-related illnesses also peak, or to a point when public willingness to endure such severe social-isolation measures had run its course. A very strange strategy indeed. Isn't it better to nip something in the bud rather than letting it grow big? If you see a few weeds in your garden, isn't it better to pull them up while they are tiny, rather than leave them to spread and grow until they are unmanageable? Didn't it occur to them that if they supressed the virus early on, they might stop it in its tracks and thus prevent a major outbreak?

Some Asian countries which experienced outbreaks before Britain nevertheless sought permanently to defeat the virus. South Korea, for example, instituted widespread testing, alongside a contact-tracing regime to keep the disease at bay until a vaccine could be found. Many others in the region adopted masks en masse. Travel restrictions were put in place. Lockdowns, large and small, were implemented . . .

Tragically the British government showed a serious lack of understanding in four main areas. Healthcare workers struggled to access personal protective equipment. Britain was too slow to implement a lockdown. Testing was grossly inadequate. Care home residents, temporarily in hospital, were sent back to their respective homes to free up beds for coronavirus victims. Many of these residents were already infected and went on to infect other residents, and staff. The death toll in care homes was horrendous.

Mr Johnson & Co claimed to have stuck closely to scientific advice. But should you follow advice blindly? Wouldn't it make sense to seek a second opinion and to use your own common sense as well?

Martin McKee, professor of European public health at the London School of Hygiene and Tropical Medicine and an adviser to the World Health Organisation says: "The countries that moved fast have curtailed the epidemic. The countries that delayed have not. It's as simple as that."

Dr Richard Horton, editor-in-chief of *The Lancet* medical journal, is even more damning, "The handling of the Covid-19 crisis in the UK is the most serious science policy failure in a generation."

By March 12 a full-scale outbreak had taken hold in Italy and the illness was spreading across Europe. More than 1,000 Italians had already died and thousands more were gravely ill in packed hospitals in the country's hard-hit north. The deadly potential of an invisible killer was becoming more obvious by the hour. But still the Johnson administration failed to take decisive action. Contact tracing was abandoned, and testing was restricted to those already in hospital with symptoms. Martine, one of Leena's former students, now a teacher in her 30s and married with two young boys, was affected by this. One day she received a phone call from her 3-year-old son's nursery to come and pick him up immediately as he had a temperature and was coughing. She rang the local hospital asking for a test, but was told that her son wasn't ill enough to be tested, but that the whole family should isolate for two weeks, which they did. It was horrendous. They had recently moved into a new house, as in newly built. There had been a lot of rain and what was to become a garden was a sea of mud, so no playing outside. Fortunately, the little boy did not get seriously ill. They all had headaches, but whether this was due to a mild attack of Covid-19 or the strain of being cooped up indoors for two weeks, they'll never know.

The Prime Minister warned at the March 12 press conference that the "worst public health crisis for a generation" was about to hit the country and that "many more families are going to lose loved ones before their time."

Early lockdown and a programme of testing would have stemmed the flow, but no such thing was implemented. Instead, people were encouraged to wash their hands and stay home for seven days if they had symptoms. Schools remained open, restaurants and bars traded as usual, and visitors were still allowed into care homes.

Flights were arriving from mainland China, even though Australia had banned them six weeks earlier. Public events such as a Champions League match in Liverpool on Mach 12 – Liverpool versus Atletico Madrid – which drew a crowd of 52,000, about 3,000 of whom came from Madrid, already on partial lockdown, was allowed to go ahead. And so was the Cheltenham horse racing festival – March 10-13, where more than 250,000 tickets were sold. Both events are being investigated by health officials who suspect they may have contributed to the rapid spread of the disease in areas surrounding the venues.

This was immediately before the weekend when Leena felt she was taking a risk by travelling to central London, and was shocked to see life going on as normal. In hindsight it has become an accepted fact by most of the population and even some scientific advisors, that this was when the powers that be should have taken Britain into lockdown. Instead they kept dithering for another week, leaving the virus to rampage through the population, destroying thousands of lives.

May 6th, 2020, Breaking News

The UK has become the first country in Europe to record 30,000 deaths from the coronavirus after it announced 649 more victims today. Now a total of 30,076 are dead because of the Covid-19 outbreak, the UK has hit the grim milestone before either Spain or Italy, which were widely considered to have the worst outbreaks in Europe. Only the US has recorded more fatalities, with 72,000.

Prime Minister Boris Johnson today admitted the situation is 'appalling' and that he 'bitterly regrets' what is happening in care homes after he was grilled by Labour leader Sir Keir Starmer, who asked, "How on Earth did it come to this?"

The rising death toll has triggered calls for an inquiry into Downing Street's handling of the crisis, with doctors accusing the Government of being too slow to start lockdown and of running an 'inadequate' testing and tracing scheme. Officials announced today that 201,101 people have now tested positive – an increase of 6,111 people today.

NHS England today confirmed 331 more people had died in hospitals. Scotland announced 83 more deaths, Wales 21 and Northern Ireland 14. It means the official count now stands at 29,876.

But the true number is thousands higher – NHS hospital statistics are still lagging behind by almost two months and one of the victims announced today actually died on March 13.

Grisly statistics released yesterday showed the true death toll had already surpassed 32,000 by April 24, meaning it could be 42 per cent higher than the official Department of Health count.

The shocking figures – compiled by the Office for National Statistics – took into account more detailed, backdated information and did not only include laboratory-confirmed cases.

It suggested Britain's real death toll may have already exceeded 40,000, meaning Covid-19 has killed more Brits in eight weeks than died over seven months during the Blitz bombings in World War II.

Much of the focus has been on Johnson: an apparent manifestation of all that has gone wrong in Britain, a caricature of imperial nostalgia, Trumpian populism, and a general lack of seriousness. Yet this was not simply an issue of political leadership, inept or otherwise: Johnson stuck closely to a strategy designed and endorsed by the government's experts, leaders in their fields and respected internationally. Even if the prime minister did make serious mistakes, the country's issues run far deeper. The British government as a whole made poorer decisions, based on poorer advice, founded on poorer evidence, supplied by poorer testing, with the inevitable consequence that it achieved poorer results than almost any of its peers. It failed in its preparation, its diagnosis and its treatment.

When the pandemic hit, Britain was not the strong, successful, resilient country it imagined, but a poorly governed and fragile one. The truth is, Britain was sick before it caught the coronavirus.

May 7th, 2020

7.19am. The sky is a luminous white. The sun has risen behind the trees on the opposite side of the road. Last night Leena took out the walnut loaf she bought in Sainsbury's on the 18th of March. It was the only bread left over from people's panic buying. She has not been short of bread, and the loaf remained forgotten in her freezer. It turned out to be delicious, and as fresh as the day it was bought.

Yesterday she was in despair about many things in the situation – a deep-seated gloom that not even a warm day under a perfect blue sky could dispel. Nor could the pleasure of discovering a new footpath through the wood between the common and the park...Continued lockdown, the coronavirus still alive and kicking. And then she read an article where a junior doctor wrote about the horror she was witnessing every day, and having to tell people that their loved-ones had died. The hopelessness of being forced to choose whose patient's hand to hold as they died, because there weren't enough doctors' and nurses' hands to go round. She described her despair about people flouting the rules of social distancing, sitting together on blankets in the park, eating, drinking, enjoying themselves as if nothing was amiss, continuing to spread the virus.

Later in the day Leena realised that lockdown might carry on for months, that the virus might be around for one or two years continuing to infect people, making the world a dangerous place. If they were all alive by the end of it, Amelia and Lea would have changed beyond recognition, and FaceTime or not, Nanny would be an irrelevance. In a long phone call Sam told her not to despair about the world, but to make the best of each day. He said the government was useless, yes, and had made grave mistakes, but what could they do about it? Leena had certainly been trying to make the best of each day, but all of a sudden it seemed so hopeless, nothing to look forward to, and what if one of them died from the virus?

She didn't say all this, but after the phone-call, she was cross with herself for having let slip her anger and frustration. She shouldn't have shown such weakness in front of her son.

But then, this morning, a short film appeared from her friend, Sandy. Five years ago, she and her husband bought a slightly rundown house – a former rectory, in East Anglia. A magical house, half-hidden behind large trees. They have never had the money to do it up, which is perhaps as well. A conservatory runs along the length of the house – old terracotta tiles on the floor, an assortment of beat-up wicker chairs with saggy cushions … Sandy had filmed a family of robins nesting in the conservatory. The film showed a fledgling darting about a trellis and some large greenery, possibly wisteria, before settling on the rim of a flower pot. It was lovely and fluffy and had not yet grown its red breast feathers. Sandy was commenting in a very quiet voice so as not to scare him, "I don't want to make him a nervous individual, for that would be awful. His mother is flying in and out through the window. She just gave him a great whopping worm, so his tummy is full … " It was a beautiful film, reminding Leena that there is still good in the world, and that's what we need to hold on to.

All the same she would have liked to venture into central London to witness the empty streets for herself, but it's too risky. She'll have to make do with Sam's descriptions.

May 11th, 2020

We'll meet gain, don't know where don't know when,
But I know we'll meet again some sunny day …

153

Vera Lynn, who passed away at the age of 103, sang these words during World War II. Suddenly today's stars, whose mothers and even grandmothers were yet to be born in 1945, are singing the famous words with renewed urgency and vigour.

*

When will Leena again visit the house in the forest? For as long as she remembers, it has been painted white, making it one with the landscape in winter. You can glimpse it from the road half-hidden behind silver birch and spruce, a private drive of some 100 metres leading up to it. Leena left it when she was young because a wider world was beckoning. She would have liked to live there now, but for various reasons it is not really feasible.

Towards the end of her mother's life, she would go there three or four times a year – weeding, raking, tidying the garden. John would mow the lawn. These days she only goes once or twice a year. During one of her most recent visits – on a day in May last year, around 6pm – she was following the footpath along the lake amid blossom and newly sprung greenery. Walking along, listening to the birdsong, she became aware of the sky; not a cloud to be seen, and the whole sky was a rich, deep yellow. The wide expanse of the lake was completely still and reflecting a perfect mirror image of the sky, as though the whole world had turned yellow. Later in the day, during the long, drawn-out Nordic dusk, the sky had changed to blood red, and so had the lake reflecting it. She was sitting on the veranda watching it, as she had done so many times before, with her mother, with John and Nina, and this time with Olav and his wife Marianne, listening to the evening breeze rustling through the birch trees – growing in strength, dying down, then growing in strength again. A spectacular sunset in the North isn't gone in a flash like it is in England. It lingers, and you can sit and watch it until all that's left is a narrow strip along the horizon. Olav and Marianne went back inside, but Leena wanted to stay a little longer, she still had a drop of white wine left in her glass. Besides, she'd soon be returning to London and there was no telling when she would next be contemplating a long and dramatic sunset. That was when she noticed that somebody was sitting in the chair just vacated by Olav. It was her mother, just sitting quietly as they had sat together during her lifetime. Neither of them saying much, watching the sunset and listening to the evening breeze blowing through the silver birches was enough. Berit's father, old Johan, had planted three birches, one for Hans, one for Leena and one for John. He hadn't specified which tree was for which child. The trees thrived. But then a strange thing happened. After Hans' disappearance they noticed that one of the birches was growing much slower than the other two. It didn't die, just stood there, hardly growing at all. Berit and August kept a keen eye on it. They had the idea that as long as the tree was alive, so was Hans, out there, somewhere. But then, a few years ago, the strangest thing had happened. The tree that had stood stunted for fifty years suddenly blossomed, and it is healthy now. Sadly, neither of her parents had lived to see it, but Leena knew that finally Hans had found happiness, wherever in the world he might be. Turned out she was right, because one frosty winter's morning she found him waiting on the doorstep with a woman at his side. Her name was Beautilill, a lovely woman, kind and gentle, a native of the Cayman Islands where Hans had been living after retiring from the sea. She had never seen snow before and was totally mesmerized. And here they sat, mother and daughter, quietly together as they had sat so many times in the past. After a while her mother said, "come on, it's getting cold, you'd better go inside." And with that she was gone.

*

For a few years Leena would visit her mother during reading week in early November – a week without lectures for students and lecturers alike to catch up on their work. But Leena did not catch up. She flew to Norway to spend the week with her mother, by then in her 80s.

On this occasion her plane had landed around 8pm, and John had picked her up from the airport train in Sandvika. By the time they were nearing the house, where Berit was waiting, it must have been after 10. As they were driving, Leena noticed the northern sky; it was bright green, like a newly mown lawn. You seldom see the aurora borealis in Southern Norway, and never as spectacular as in the North. But sometimes, on a late-autumn night, you get an echo of it, and this was such a night. Leena had seen a green night sky before, but never as bright as this and she said to John: "Can you stop a minute. I'd like to try to take a picture of the sky." She'd been a keen photographer since she was 12, and always carried a camera in her handbag. But John replied,

"No, better not, Mum is waiting, and if we are late, she'll start worrying. You know what she's like."

*

Leena's original plan had been to spend a week in Norway round about now, and then another week towards the end of summer. The May visit is not going to happen, obviously, and very likely neither is the visit planned for late August. Will she sit on the veranda watching a sunset or see black spruces silhouetted against a green night sky ever again? She can only hope.

*

Etched on her brain is another memory, this one form February 16th this year. Normally she wouldn't remember the precise date, but this time she does, because it marked the end of her last visit to Berlin for God knows how long. Allan and Amelia had accompanied her by train to Hauptbahnhof where she would board a bus for Tegel Airport. Amelia was hungry, and Leena had bought her a pretzel, popular fast food all over Germany. The ticket machines in Berlin are a major challenge. On every platform, you see people, especially tourists, struggling with them. There are just too many alternatives, none very clear. Like with most electronics, easy when you know how, near impossible when you don't. Very likely you can get an around the world ticket, if only you knew how. You finally think you've worked it out, only to discover that what you thought would give you a simple one-day ticket will set you back €34, which can't be right. So, none the wiser, you start again, painfully aware of the queue forming behind you. If you are lucky, somebody in the queue will help you, or point you towards a hidden-away window where a live human will sell you the right ticket. Allan normally has this under control, but on this day the machine would not work. Or, perhaps there simply wasn't an option for a single bus-ticket to the airport. Leena gave Allan some change. Being a modern man, he hardly ever carries cash, and off he went in search of a different machine or an elusive human ticket-seller. Some ten minutes later, he returned with the ticket and one spare euro, which Leena gave to Amelia for pocket money, and she was pleased. After that, they walked with her across the square to where the airport bus would be stopping. It soon arrived, and Leena got on. She waved to them through the window – Allan in his navy winter coat and Amelia in her yellow quilted coat and navy woolly hat, still eating her pretzel, smiling and waving back at her – the unemotional goodbye of people who will soon be seeing each other again. In the meantime, Allan's work would take him to London for a couple of days. Now Leena is thinking that if it hadn't been for this impromptu visit because of Elida's illness, they wouldn't even have had these few days together. Allan's business trip to London had to be cancelled, and if or when they will see each other again is totally up in the air.

*

Berlin is not the easiest city in which to learn your way about. There doesn't seem to be a central feature to orient yourself from. London has the Thames, Trafalgar Square, Piccadilly Circus, the Mall and Buckingham Palace, even Oxford Street...Wherever you are, at least around the centre, there will be somewhere familiar close by. Budapest have the Danube. Prague has the Vltava. Oslo has Karl Johans Street running through the centre from the Royal Palace to Central Station, passing the National Theatre and the Norwegian Parliament building (Stortinget). In Budapest, for example, she would work her way to the Danube and walk along it until she came to Freedom Bridge, where she would turn right or left, depending on which direction she came from, soon to find herself in the familiar streets around Sam's block. Berlin doesn't seem to have any one such feature. The river Spree meanders its way through the city, but not in a clear line like the Thames or the Seine. Alexander Platz with the TV Tower is perhaps the closest you get to a central feature. There is Museum Island passed by trams and trains and of course the Brandenburg Gate, but nothing, to Leena's mind as clear-cut as the Thames, Seine, Karl Johans or the Danube.

Yes, it must be the TV Tower. Leena can't see what else it could be. She remembered it well from her first visit

159

back in 2013. But never had she thought that one day she would have lunch in the revolving restaurant high up in the ball, nor did she particularly want to. It wasn't the height that frightened her, it was the thought of taking the lift all the way up the thin windowless tube to get up there.

It happened like this. For a while Allan had a Californian business associate who was visiting Berlin with his wife and young daughter at the same time as Leena. It was summer and they'd all had a meal together. The business associate, Raymond Broom, told them that he had booked a table for them all at the revolving restaurant in the tower the following day. It was more of a summons than an invitation. Amelia and Lea were in their respective nurseries. Elida had to work, so it ended up being just Leena and Allan. Raymond's wife and nine-year-old daughter came too. Once they got to the Tower and saw all the people milling about the souvenir shop and going up in the lift, the scene looked so normal that Leena lost her fear of the 200 metres' high lift-shaft. The sun was shining and there was a holiday atmosphere, naturally enough, as most of the visitors were tourists. The lift was roomier and faster than expected, so it didn't feel frightening at all. Allan and Leena assumed that as Raymond had invited them, he would also pay. But they had to pay for themselves, right down to the last cent; tickets to get up there and the meal, which was surprisingly unimpressive. Leena had a pasta dish which looked and tasted as though it had been sitting around for a while. Allan has since broken off his connection with Raymond as he was not quite the hotshot he affected to be, although they still see each other from time to time. Yet, it certainly was an enjoyable event – seeing a different view each time you looked out of the window, and an experience Leena is unlikely to have had, if it hadn't been for a charlatan called Raymond Broom.

*

Leena has no sense of direction. So, finding her way around a new city is a struggle. Even after multiple visits, Berlin still has not quite emerged from the mist of falling leaves.

So, trying to get used to Berlin, she started at ground level. Which meant local shops, the nearest tram-stop, and the way to Amelia's nursery, at first an ignominy as far as Amelia was concerned, having already been to proper school on Grand Cayman. However, finding the other kids in her group being the same age as her, she soon accepted it. The way to her nursery or kita – the German term for kinder garden – was quite simple: two stops with the M10 tram, across a busy street where there ought to have been a traffic light, but wasn't, and then straight ahead for 7-8 minutes. After that simple enough but still with plenty of room for error for someone with no sense of direction. Leena knew she'd got it right when, first, passing a park on the right-hand side of the street, she then saw the ice-cream parlour in the distance. Going back, retracing her steps ought to have been easy, but Leena still managed to get it wrong a couple of times. People with a normal sense of direction simply have no idea! In those early days she had Lea in her buggy. On the way home they would stop for an ice-cream along with other adults and kids from the kita, a friendly place with a good choice of ice-cream and tables inside and out. Leena would feed Lea bits of her own ice-cream with a plastic spoon. After that off to the tram-stop and home. One summer's day they came across a wooden box with several bouquets of beautiful flowers in a bucket of water. Leena assumed they were there for people to help themselves, and looking closer she discovered a note which said to leave 2 euros in the letterbox. The bouquets were all slightly different. They chose one, left the 2 euros and continued on their way. When Elida got back from work, she was pleased to find the flowers. Next time Leena passed, she looked through a crack in the tall wooden fence, and saw a garden brimming with flowers. One day she even happened by as an elderly, Indian-looking lady was putting them out. Leena told her how she loved seeing her flowers and that she often bought a bunch.

May 12th, 2020

Another morning of pure white sky and brilliant sunshine, but cold. No wind. Yesterday was partly cloudy and with an icy blustery wind.

Boris Johnson spoke to the nation on Sunday. Today is Tuesday 12th. Leena sometimes has to look at the calendar to make sure she has the correct day and date. That's what happens when each day is without distinguishing features. Although there is always something. Yesterday at

7.30pm they were having an online choir practice again, still struggling with the Elijah Choruses. It went quite well. The first time it was a shambles with everybody singing at different speeds. It has been a learning process for everyone, including Nancy. A few adjustments have been made and it's now going quite well. Although, being in the grips of a pestilence, the choice of repertoire is rather too close to home.

Especially Chorus no 1:
Lord! Wilt Thou quite destroy us?
Or, Chorus no 5:
He mocketh at us, his curse has fallen down upon us;
His wrath will pursue us till he destroys us.

The same sentences repeated again and again. Leena is not religious. Still, the thought of divine retribution has crossed her mind. The Old Testament prophet, Elijah, was referring to a drought that threatened people's lives, but there is a parallel with the present situation. True; this alarming music was chosen before Covid-19 changed our lives. However, Nancy finds it beautiful, or rather grand, but still ... She spends her life in the colourful world of opera, so perhaps the harsh lines don't affect her the way they affect Leena and some other choir members.

What else? She talked to Allan in the morning. She told him that Amelia's birthday present which she had bought online had arrived as promised, and she would wrap it up nicely and send it to Berlin. Yesterday Sam wanted to make his way across London by Tube to see her, but then he wasn't feeling very well, so he decided to come today instead. Leena loves seeing him, but hates the

163

idea of him getting infected on the Tube, although there is a 90% chance that he has had, and recovered from the virus. It is, however, not clear how much immunity it might have given him ...

And so, the day continued.

*

Back to Boris and his address to the nation. He seemed in good shape and started by pointing out that a lot has been achieved through social isolation. Without it the death toll would have been a lot worse, he mentioned half a million. In view of this, easing the measures now, would quickly undo what has been achieved. He forgot to mention that the number of dead would have been a lot lower if only he and his cronies had got their act together and started lockdown a week before. Perhaps restrictions could be eased in June. They would have to keep monitoring the situation. Impossible to give a timetable for coming out of lockdown at this stage. All logical and sensible, Leena thought, even though she is no fan of Mr Johnson. Then followed details of which groups should try to get back to work, if they had to. They should as far as possible avoid public transport and walk, ride a bike or drive.

The address was followed by interviews with some ordinary people to gauge their reaction. Some of them were incensed, devastated, disappointed (their own words). They appeared to have believed that lockdown would come to an end and everything would return to normal, talking as though the government had robbed them of their freedom for no good purpose. They wanted a precise timetable for coming out of lockdown, but how could that be possible when it all depends on what happens about the virus? It's bizarre! What do people think with? If they wanted everything to suddenly open up, they have not understood a thing.

But today is another day. Sam may or may not come. The magnolia tree outside her window is covered in dense foliage. A few pink flowers poking out in between, latecomers, soon to disappear. Instead the roses are coming out. One more week and they'll be in full bloom.

Breaking News

Ryanair set to restore 40% of normal flight schedule from July 1st, with crew and passengers wearing facemasks, and passengers having to ask the attendants to use the toilets which will be locked.

There you are. Before too long thousands of airplanes will again be criss-crossing the sky, polluting the air which has been so much cleaner since lockdown. What little has been achieved for the planet will soon be reversed. Too many people worldwide depend on the polluters for their everyday living, in the same way as low-income people make do with cheap unhealthy food. It keeps them fed from one day to the next, but in the long run it shortens their lives. A crying shame, for who, in the present crisis have kept the wheels of society running if not people of low income? At least they should be able to afford decent food. The planet too deserves better than what modern civilisation is doing to it.

May 13th, 2020

The day is overcast and quite cold with a wind from the north. Sam has finally said he is definitely coming. Leena is cooking a prawn and mushroom curry with new potatoes and fresh coriander leaves.

Sam arrived at 3.30, having picked up some shopping for her on the way. All the time keeping at two metres' distance. After the meal they went for a walk across the common and through the park. On her own Leena can barely stand it, same old, same old – across the wide grassy plane of the common, then through the wood, beautiful, but much too tiny, then across the road and into the park. Leena knows she is privileged to have such expansive green spaces close by. Even so, it gets too samey, fine when she is walking with Sam, but on her own it is becoming more about exercise and less about enjoying nature. As always, it's hard not to talk about the present situation as everything else seems irrelevant. Now they are talking about how neither of them has ever experienced a real catastrophe, not even Leena. Never has she lived through a calamity that could go on for years.

Their thoughts go to June last year when they spent six days in an Airbnb in Neukölln. Further away from Allan and family than they wanted, but having left the booking a bit late, it was the best they could find. Neukölln is a pleasant district, once part of the American sector and situated just south of Kreuzberg. It is home to a strong immigrant community, mainly Turkish, but other ethnicities as well. Like Friedrichshain and Kreuzberg it appeals to students, artists and intellectuals and is therefore subject to gentrification.

They were there to celebrate Amelia's 6th birthday on June 4th. Unbelievable as it now seems, less than a year ago. How different everything was back then. All the photos show happy and smiling faces. People having fun, enjoying Amelia's special day. Elida looking radiant and beautiful.

Now things have changed. Being a sociable person, Elida finds that the strain of not seeing her friends is getting to her. Add to that not being able to send the children to school and nursery. Amelia has structured home school, where she is in contact with her teachers and the rest of her class. Fortunately, she enjoys her schoolwork and seeing her class, all-be-it on a screen. Her parents take it in turns to stay home and look after the girls. Elida goes to work twice a week in an office especially adapted for social distancing. Allan has an office to himself and goes in two or three days a week. But, with two children around all day, one of them too young to understand, the confinement is beginning to take its toll.

*

Their Airbnb was within walking distance of the disused Tempelhof Airport, once the site of Nazi rallies and the airlift bringing vital supplies to West Berlin during 1948–49. It was one of Europe's iconic pre-World War II airports, the others being London's now defunct Croydon Airport and the old Paris–Le Bourget Airport, and was one of the earliest commercial airports in the world. Tempelhof ceased operating in 2008, leaving Tegel and Schönefeld as the two main airports serving the city, with the new Berlin Brandenburg Airport still under construction. Tempelhof is now designated as a gigantic park/recreation ground for Berliners to enjoy–an enormous open space with the runway still intact, no trees. Sam and Leena walked there one sunny day through streets lined with pleasant little shops, greengrocers and cafés, most of them run by Turkish people. From where they entered the park, they could see the old airport buildings in the distance. A very peaceful place, difficult to think that it had once played host to gigantic Nazi rallies, and large aircraft thundering along. There was a kiosk, and deckchairs set out. They bought two cans of coconut-water, and sat down on the chairs. Being used to London's parks, they expected somebody to come and ask them to pay for using the chairs, but no such thing happened, and they understood that they were free. It was a normal weekday, but still there was a fair number of people about. People of all ages were cycling on the old runway. Others were jogging or just walking. A remnant of the past transformed into a treasure of today, like being back in a kinder and more tranquil world.

*

Leena has seen far from enough of Berlin to give an informed opinion based on her own observations. However, it seems to her that the glass and concrete constructions so proudly shown off by the tourist guide back in 2013 are only a small part of the picture. The real Berlin is old and saturated with memories of the past. Take Friedrichshain for example. In 2018 Sam and Leena spent Christmas with Allan and family. On Christmas Day Leena had gone out to buy milk from one of the little shops that always seems to be open. Walking back, it suddenly struck her that there was nothing to indicate that it was Christmas, nothing. No colourful lights, no Christmas trees, no decorations in the shop windows, or in people's windows. The tattooed youngsters were nowhere to be seen. Only a few old souls out walking their dogs, closed up faces, some of them shabbily dressed. Very likely they had lived here all their lives, and survived 40 years of communism. Stripped of its modern inhabitants, it was like stepping back in time – the modest little shops, the bars and restaurants … Wash away the graffiti and street art and you find yourself in a different time, a time void of colour and light, as pointed out by one of Elida's friends who grew up in East Berlin. She was only a child at the time and living under the yoke of communism hadn't meant anything to her. Life was life – playing in the courtyard with other kids, their mothers calling them in for dinner … The reunification didn't mean much to her either, except that suddenly there were colours, bright, shiny colours everywhere.

Leena never visited East Berlin during the communist period. She has friends who had been there. One of them, a woman called Traute, she used to see a lot of back in the 1970s and 80s, said that the place had given her the creeps, and there were tanks in the streets.

Charles, Leena's friend from UCL days, told her about a trip he'd made to Berlin in April 1989, which still sticks in his mind.

His girlfriend's sister, Katrina, had driven him there from Hanover with another friend. The trip involved a drive in the dark through 200km of pine forests along one of the designated transit routes, the only sign of civilisation being the lights from Magdeburg in the distance at one point.

In the middle of the trip they stopped in a layby to stretch their legs. Charles came back to the small car with the impression that the wood was haunted. Katrina laughed, "Those weren't ghosts! They were Stasi checking that West Germans weren't leaving things in the woods for their Eastern relatives."

Shortly after a sign for "Berlin, Hauptstadt der Deutschen Demokratsichen Republik [Berlin, Capital of the GDR] 50km", all hell broke loose. They were suddenly driving fast on a brightly lit autobahn on the edge of West Berlin. It would have taken them 50km to get around to the Capital; in fact, they were already in West Berlin.

Then typical German side streets, passing a power station at one point. "Oh yes; there was a grand plan to use it to supply hot water to the houses for heating, but something blew up and that was that."

They were based in Amrumer Straße in the North and Charles spent the next day exploring West Berlin. All the facilities of a capital city, but calm, as there were few people.

The following day, Katrina said, "I need some candles. Let's go to East Berlin. They're cheap there and very good." And so, they got the S-Bahn to Friedrichstraße. After they left Lehrter Stadt Station, in the West. (Lehrter Stadt Station no longer exists but the present Hauptbahnhof is built on the same site.) From there, they looked down into the death strip to the east. When they went downstairs at Friedrichstraße, the guards called Charles' name three times to check his identity. The atmosphere was very tense. They got the S-Bahn to Alexander Platz and bought the candles at the department store there and then went to a bookshop. They queued to get a basket to go in, they queued to get tickets for their books and they queued to pay. Charles said the books on linguistics were of a high standard. The maps of Germany were useless, though, as West Berlin was a white blob.

They went to the Pergamon and admired the Babylonian altar. Charles brushed a display case and there was a voice immediately, "Bitte nicht berühren!" [Please don't touch!]

The streets were drab, no adverts and everything seemed to be GDR black, dirty white, green, brown or orange.

171

Charles and Katrina had a cheap lunch of pineapple chicken and Berliner Weiße mit Schuss, wheat bear in a bowl-shaped glass with a shot of raspberry or a green liquid Charles has since discovered is artificial woodruff flavouring, whatever that is, in the Palast der Republik. A GDR prestige project – the parliament building with its dark glass and spherical lights high on the ceiling. Since demolished as it was riddled with asbestos. It was on the site of the old Schloss, which has since been reconstructed.

After lunch, they split up. Katrina had something else to do, but Charles decided he wouldn't explore on his own and got the S-Bahn back from Friedrichstraße. Nobody would have guessed that the Wall would have come down by the end of the year. Charles has felt a link to this craziest of cities ever since.

Leena's experiences with Berlin are nowhere near as dramatic, in fact, they are not dramatic at all. Still, Berlin has something that can never be eradicated. Peel away the high-rise blocks, the graffiti and the tattooed youngsters and you're back in the 1920s, 50s or 70s, a time where the 21st century has yet to take hold.

May 16th, 2020

Three months to the day since she waved goodbye to Allan and Amelia at Hauptbahnhof in Berlin, thinking she'd see them again in five weeks' time. Two months and a day since her last foray up to London before lockdown. She would like to go there now, simply to get the feel of the deserted streets, but Sam won't have it. He is fiercely protective of her health, and she doesn't want to go there and not tell him. That would be too dishonest, especially as he travels all the way across London to bring her stuff, mainly goodies from M&S plus heavy and bulky things that, in the old world, she would take home on the bus. These days Sam won't hear of her using public transport. She could catch the virus. Not everybody keeps a safe distance. She has no control over who might plonk themselves down just behind her and start coughing. Sam probably has some immunity, at least they hope so. Another example of the shambolic government: there are no tests available for the man in the street, and only now are they beginning seriously to test health-care workers to see if they have had the virus.

Onal next door brings her things too, and Angie and Ray two doors away. Leena and Angie used to go for a meal once a month or so, but no chance of that now. Leena introduced her to Thai food and she loves it. Anyway, she doesn't want her neighbours to stay longer in a shop than necessary on her account, and only asks them for things that are easy to find, and only when they come and ask if she needs anything. With Sam she can be more specific. She could easily nip down to Sainsbury Local at the end of the road, and sometimes she does, always with a face mask. The shop is not bad, but being much smaller than an ordinary supermarket, it's somewhat limited. Before Easter, Ray power-cleaned her decking and patio. It took him nearly all day. Such good neighbours, all of them, except the ogre. However, there is now a possibility that he's gone for good.

Some days she can't help but feel negative – sitting around the house, pottering about the garden, living the life of a much older person. If Leena feels angry about anything, it is that the virus may rob her of precious years of vitality. Healthwise there is no reason why she shouldn't go about her life like she's always done. But no, the virus is out there, and will be for a long time to come. It may have taken away her freedom of movement, but so far it has not ended her life, so better stop complaining. It may sound superficial, but she misses smartening herself up and going somewhere, meeting up with somebody – something to look forward to.

Three days ago, something finally happened. The ogre might be dead. He was a member of the local Rotary Club. He did not answer the phone when the chairman rang him about something or other, and the chairman got worried, fearing he had caught the virus. As there was no reply the following morning, he went to his house and rang the doorbell. Still no reaction. He couldn't peer through the windows as the ogre always kept his blinds tightly drawn, so he called the police. Whilst waiting, he asked Leena, who happened to be in the garden, when she had last seen him. She replied that come to think of it, she hadn't seen him for a couple of days. That was it. Suddenly there was a police car and an emergency ambulance. Two police officers, with face masks and gloves on, managed to open the front door. Three paramedics entered. Leena was surprised to see that they had no protective gear except the gloves and face masks. Apart from that, ordinary navy trousers and T-shirts. Shouldn't they have proper protective equipment when entering the house of a potential corona victim? The policemen asked Leena and other neighbours who had gathered, to go back into their homes. They did as they were told, but unwilling to miss out on the excitement, they took up position at their respective windows. The police soon left, but the paramedics remained inside for quite some time. One of them came out and fetched a wheelchair from the ambulance. Leena wanted to make herself a cup of coffee, but didn't like to leave the window in case they brought out the ogre while she was in the kitchen – dead or alive, she had to know. After about half an hour, the paramedics left the house, the ogre slumped in the wheelchair, blanket over his knees, an oxygen mask covering his face, obviously unwell, but definitely not dead. The paramedics now wore plastic aprons in addition to their gloves and face masks, living proof of the scandalous shortage of PPE. Five minutes later the ambulance drove off, no blue lights or sirens. So, not too serious then.

Denise Brown, his neighbour on the other side, had talked to the Rotary member, when he came round to check the house the following day, and been told that the ogre had suffered a heart attack and had been on the floor for 24 hours, unable to get up.

And now he has been in hospital for four days. Leena's phone rang. It was Angie. She wondered if she had seen the ambulance parked outside the ogre's house. "You have a better view than me, could you see what's going on?" Leena got to her window just in time to see two

175

paramedics slowly walking the ogre back into his house, each holding him by the crook of his arm.

So, there you have it. The ogre will live to grumble another day. And the monotony of lockdown has turned two educated ladies – Angie is a preschool teacher – into avid sensation-seekers.

*

The day before lockdown Leena had the forethought to go to the garden centre at the bottom of her road to buy pansies and compost, as much as she could carry. She loves that garden centre. It is a beautiful and peaceful place and has a tiny pond with large, bright-red koi. It is well visited, although some people complain that it is too expensive. But so what? The pleasure of going there instead of to a huge DIY outfit is worth a few extra pounds. Besides, she believes in supporting local businesses. Leena bought blue and yellow pansies, as they were the only spring flowers available, and divided them between five large pots along her front wall. They looked lonely at first, but it didn't take them long to fill the pots, and now passers-by comment on how nice they look.

This week they opened the garden centre again, and Leena went there yesterday, face mask at the ready. She doesn't wear it when walking about with plenty of space around her, only when she's inside a shop or the post office. There was a long queue, two metres' distance between each person. When Leena finally reached the entrance, the employee guarding the door asked her what she had come for. She replied, begonias, and he pointed to where to find them. Clearly, they didn't want people hanging about, taking their time, looking at this and that, unable to decide what they wanted, or perhaps wanting nothing at all. They didn't have a lot of begonias, and she bought eight red ones and three white. She wanted to plant some on Tom's grave as well. There was no potting compost to be had, so she would have to make do with what was left over in the pots from last year.

*

Before leaving for the garden centre, she must have forgotten to turn off her radio, because as she entered, they were playing *Sanctus* from *The Armed Man, a Hymn to Peace* by Karl Jenkins, a most powerful movement. It starts with a dramatic drum-beat mimicking the sound of marching soldiers. The drumbeat, although sometimes only heard in the background, continues throughout the movement, keeping up the effect. In 2018 her choir performed *The Armed Man* at their spring concert on April 14th. How wonderful it was to be part of such a performance. Leena can't believe that it was just over two years ago. Hearing the music now made her think of happier days when fantastic things were taken for granted. How different everything was back them. You could plan things and be fairly confident that they would happen. The years had their rhythm: Christmas concert, spring concert, summer concert, rehearsed and performed year after year, regular as clockwork, only the exact dates changed from one year

177

to the next. And in between … visits to Norway, visits to Budapest, visits to the Cayman Islands and later to Berlin, visits to her friend, Victoria in Oxford …

*

January 2020 started like every January with rehearsals for the spring concert on April 4th. This year they were performing Beethoven's beautiful Mass in C, as it was his 250th anniversary. Difficult in parts, they had worked hard to get it right. They all felt sad when the concert had to be cancelled and rehearsals discontinued. The summer concert was always in doubt because of lockdown. However, Nancy kept nursing a hope that it might still miraculously go ahead, and set up online rehearsals. This too, regrettably, seems unrealistic. And the Christmas concert … who knows?

There are people who have been through worse than a couple of cancelled concerts. She has to hope that some day in the future there will be other performances, and that she will still be able to take part. Last time she spoke to Amelia on FaceTime, she said she wanted to come to her concert and hear Nanny sing. Let's hope it will happen. One can't plan, but one can hope.

May 22nd, 2020

Another morning of luminous white sky. Only one lone flower left on the magnolia tree. The roses are in full bloom, yellow, white, pink, red, some of the bushes two metres tall. The begonias she planted a few days ago are doing well. Don't ask her on which day – Tuesday, Wednesday, Thursday – days drift by, slowly merging into one. Very little to tell them apart. She has noticed nurses coming and going at the ogre's house. No PPE. Dandelions are beginning to sprout between the paving-stones on his patio.

The 18th was her birthday. Angie brought her a pot of miniature cala lilies and a card. Another friend, Niki, sent her a pot of gorgeous pink lilies. They appeared at her door, quite unexpectedly. Amelia and Lea sang their arrangement of happy birthday on FaceTime. She received loads of messages. Sam arrived bringing risotto that he had cooked at home, still warm. As a child and youngster, he hadn't shown much interest in food and cooking, but over the years he has developed into a competent cook. He brought her a large bunch of red and pink roses and white lilies, and a card of course.

A kind day. After lunching on Sam's risotto, a recipe with white wine and parmesan, they went for a walk, first around the common, then through the park, same as on Sam's birthday. Leena has never been athletic, but she enjoys walking. When she lived in Norway, she would walk or cycle everywhere. You can think when you walk or cycle, notice flowers, take in a beautiful view. Better than whizzing through the landscape with your eyes glued to the road. Once in Norway she saw a baby badger in the long grass by the roadside. She had never seen a badger before, and stood watching it for ages.

Sam too enjoys walking, and to a lesser extent Allan, a mixture of nature and nurture. One summer, after walking all day in the Norwegian mountains, she and 16-year-old Sam, spent the night in a remote lodge with no electricity, except for a limited generator. There was a bathroom. To have a shower you had to insert a five kroner coin, around 50p, into a slot by the shower. When the five kroner ran out, so did the hot water. In the morning they woke up to what sounded like pigs grunting. They looked out and saw a flock of wild reindeer feasting on heather and mountain grass right outside the window, at least 20 animals, some only half grown. The sun had just risen above the mountain, and the air was crisp and clear. You'll never get to see a sight like that by whizzing through the landscape on a motorway, your aim being to get from A to B as quickly as possible.

Having reached the park, they spent some time sitting on separate benches, about two metres apart. There were more people about than on Sam's birthday, but the ice-cream van still had not turned up. Another small business fallen by the wayside, most likely. Some 30 metres away from them a family group – mother, father, granny and two kids out on a picnic – were about to leave, packing away their bits and pieces, gathering toddler and five-year-old, leaving behind a pile of rubbish on the grass. Sam said, "I can't stand this" and off he went to talk to them. Leena didn't like it, but Sam is a karate brown belt, and for a while he did kick boxing, so he is not lacking in confidence. He went up to the group, nicely and politely and said, "Excuse me, but I think you forgot something."

The three adults looked at him, "Did we? What did we forget?"

Sam, "Your rubbish, you forgot to take your rubbish."

The man blew himself up like an angry cockerel. For a moment Leena worried it might come to blows, but then the wife said, "Come on, let's pick it up." And off she went, filling a plastic bag with empty bottles and what have you, the granny helping, the man glaring at Sam who said, as politely as before, "There's a bin down there where you can put it."

And off they went, the man muttering between his teeth, but loud enough for them to hear, "Bloody toffs!"

Back at the house around 7. Sam had brought cheese-cake with berries, Leena's favourite, rather than a traditional birthday cake. He had even thought of candles. It had been a wonderful birthday, better than a party with friends, because friends come and go over the years. Much better then, to spend the day with someone who really matters to you.

*

It's been decided. No concert on July 4th. The church where it was supposed to have taken place has cancelled all events until September.

Yesterday she read the following **Breaking News:** *EasyJet will resume flights from some airports in Britain, France and Spain from June 15 – with all passengers and crew told to wear face masks.* So far, no planes to Berlin, but it will come. Berlin has not been too badly hit by the virus and now it is on its way to being eradicated altogether. Perhaps she will get to see her loved-ones in Berlin before the end of summer after all.

*

Late afternoon. Outside the sun is shining and a lively wind is making the trees perform joyous dances as if to music, making you happy to be alive. In a moment Leena will walk down to Sainsbury Local and the garden centre to see what she can find. Sam has just texted asking for the recipe for her special chilli bean dish. Allan will probably ring later today, and if not today, then tomorrow. At 8 she'll watch *The World's Most Scenic Railway Journeys, Mexico.* Life in lockdown goes on, until further notice, whenever that might be.

So here she sits, scribbling in her notebook. The red pen she bought in the Harry Potter shop at Gatwick on the 11th of February, en route to Berlin, is still going strong, weighing heavily in her hand, a tangible memento of a happy day when life was normal. That's what we need – a parallel world of wizards and witches and owls instead of e-mails – a magical world where fantastic things can happen, if only we could find it.

May 24th, 2020

Another beautiful morning. The sky is pale blue with a few wisps of peach-coloured clouds. Less than a month until summer solstice. The roses are at their most glorious and the magnolia tree has shed its last bloom. A large fly is buzzing around the window. Irritating, and a sure sign that summer is on its way. Leena opens the window to let it out, but stupidly it retreats further into the room.

For nearly three months she's been spending most of her time around the house, never venturing further than she can get to on foot – watching winter give way to spring and spring to summer. But apart from nature doing what nature does, her life has been at a standstill, as if locked in a capsule whilst around her life goes on as normal. And the weather – uninterrupted sunshine all day long, day after day – in a country used to constant changes – enhances the feeling of being trapped in a motionless world. If only she could find a way out . . .

*

There is a nature reserve a couple of miles from Leena's house, a vast area where the grass is never cut, and flowers, weeds and trees are allowed to grow as they please. There is a lake too, and footpaths and cycle lanes leading through forests and meadows. For Leena, missing the Norwegian wilderness, a tiny taste of home. However, it took her a long time to give it a try. It looked dark and deserted, not the sort of place a woman would venture into on her own. When she finally plucked up the courage to go there, she found it less empty than she had feared, and lighter. There were dog-walkers, people on bikes and mothers with children cutting through on their way from school.

Yesterday, for the first time in months, she made her way to the reserve. Getting there, without the use of transport, is a bit of a challenge, starting with a walk down a seemingly endless street of 1930s houses, semi-detached or in rows of four, decent enough but nothing special. After that, past two up-market restaurants, one Indian and one Italian, both of them now closed. Then past a row of little shops and a chippy, which appears to be open. After that past a florist-cum-café, also closed. A popular place where she would sometimes go for a coffee with her friends, Patsy and Mike. Last time she spoke to them, they told her that their daughter, Karen, a doctor working with corona patients is well, but doesn't want to see them. She worries that she might be a carrier and give them the virus. The road carries on past a car showroom and a pub with a large outdoor seating area, closed, but the tables are still out. Further along there is a big Tesco where she has to negotiate a major junction.

It's just after midday and already hot. She regrets her choice of clothes – red jeans and a matching T-shirt with ¾ length sleeves. She should have worn something lighter, but she has a craving for red, it's a cheerful colour and always makes her feel better about things.

Finally, there. How wonderfully cool … straight into what looks like a deep forest but only continues for five minutes before you come to a wide meadow, covered in cow parsley, white against a background of deep-green trees. And above it all, the sky – looking more infinite and bluer than Leena has ever seen it around London – a few white woolly clouds. Totally worth the dreary walk to get here. A lot of people about, cycling or walking. Lockdown has not only made the air cleaner. It seems to have made people appreciate the treasures on their doorstep as well. And this glorious panorama is what the government wanted to deny her, simply because she was born a year too soon, making her old and decrepit and vulnerable, to be isolated and locked in her home for four months for her own protection, at least that's what they said. A woman with dreadlocks well below her waist, and a beautiful huge dog on a lead, smiles, and remarks as she passes in the opposite direction, "At least now we're allowed out."

Leena replies, "I used to go out anyway, who was to stop me?"

The woman, "Precisely, sitting indoors would have driven me mad."

Still, the woman, who didn't look a day over 65, would have been all right. People of 70+ were allowed out to walk their dogs. Then again, it might not be her dog. A middle-aged couple on bikes ask Leena if she knows where the lake is, and she points them in the right direction. Hidden between trees, you don't see it before it's right in front of you.

Having brought water and sandwiches and a bar of chocolate, Leena makes her way to the lake, hoping to find a secluded spot where she can enjoy her lunch, and for a bench to sit on. She finds a spot with no people, but no bench, so she sits down on the ground. How beautiful it is – the water absolutely still, the only ripples caused by a swan and her signets. And along the shore, dense watergrass, flowering brambles and yellow irises. A woman with two young children and a black French bull terrier come along. The dog immediately takes a shine to Leena, or perhaps it's her sandwiches. She feeds him a few crusts which he devours and begs for more. They get talking. The woman says she likes Leena's accent, and asks where she comes from. She tells Leena that after 40 years in Britain she has ended up sounding completely British even though she is nothing of the sort. Her father is from Ghana and her mother is German, but now she has all but forgotten her German. She doesn't even look 40, so she can't have been very old when she arrived here, no wonder she has a perfect British accent. A lovely encounter. And, what Johnson & Co would have denied her, if they'd had their way.

May 27th, 2020

Then there is the saga of Dominic Cummings, the PM's chief advisor who on March 31st drove from London to Durham, because he and his wife were suffering from coronavirus symptoms, so that his parents could look after their four-year-old son. A drive totally disregarding government guidelines that stated: *You should not be visiting family members who do not live in your home. Those in a household with symptoms must 'stay at home and not leave the house' for up to 14 days.*

The journey came to light and all hell broke loose: one law for the likes of Mr Cummings, and one for the rest of the population. People would be thinking: if Mr Cummings can flout the regulations, why not me? By doing what he did, Mr Johnson's right-hand man was spitting in the faces of the NHS workers risking their lives every day, as well as people who had declined to see their stricken loved-ones because of the regulations. That was how many people saw it. Would there now be a new wave of Covid-19 incidents because of people flouting regulations? And why did the PM defend him? Was it because Mr Cummings is really running the country and Mr Johnson is lost without him? The furore went on and on and still does. Mr Cummings made excuses and gave reasons why. The nation was shocked on Sunday afternoon when the PM stood up and defended him. But then how could he sack a man who had helped him to push through Brexit, and said to be the brain behind slogans like, *Get Brexit done. Give us back our country. Let's show them what Britain can do.* Cheap slogans that appealed to the masses without a word of how?

And about the five-hour drive to Durham with his four-year-old child locked in a car with both parents with coronavirus symptoms. Didn't they know that there was a chance their child might catch the virus and be a carrier without displaying any symptoms? Perhaps the idea that a child could be a silent carrier had not yet become general knowledge, but it was still a risky thing to do. And what about Mr Cummings' parents who looked after the child? With a 48-year-old son they must surely be the age of people termed vulnerable and to be isolated in their homes. So, shouldn't his elderly parents be protected rather than being responsible for a child who might well infect them with the virus?

*

Lockdown in England has been eased. People are allowed out for longer periods of time and to talk to friends and relations as long as they stick to social distancing. As feared by many, the bank holiday weekend saw people flocking to beaches, and not much sign of social distancing. Who knows where that might lead?

And now people in England are allowed to meet up in groups of up to six, as long as they stick to the two metres' distance rule. But will it work? Some people are bound to think if six people are allowed why not seven, and if seven, perhaps we can get away with eight? And as for distancing, even with the best will, old habits will take over and without people realising it, two metres will have shrunk to one, and then back to normal ...

The government is introducing a tracking app that will tell if somebody has been near a person with coronavirus. The person will be informed, and told to isolate for 14 days, and also asked to reveal who he/she has been in contact with, so that they can also be tracked and told to isolate. A test and trace method that has worked in other countries. But in Britain, the planning of it all seems rather shambolic. The press now has the knives out for Mr Johnson. One paper reported that when asked, he did not appear to know how the tracking system works.

What many people can't understand, Leena among them, is this absolute refusal on the part of Messrs Johnson and Cummings to admit that Cummings' actions were wrong, or at least ill-considered. An admission along the following of, "In hindsight I can see that what I did was thoughtless and rash. I should have found a different solution to our childcare problem, and I am sorry about any upset and distress I might have caused," would have gone some way towards remedying the situation. But apparently, Mr Cummings is perfect. He makes no mistakes.

One thing is for certain, Mr Johnson's government is a government in crisis. 61 Conservative MPs have refused to back him in his plea to move on from the Cummings crisis. We can only hope that the British public has more common sense than people in power, who appear to have very little.

One must not confuse a country's people with its leaders. Most people are decent and sensible and go about their lives as best they can. Pragmatic, well-meaning and polite, qualities that will see Britain through its deepening crisis, however long it might take.

May 29th, 2020

Another sunny day in England's green and pleasant land. Yesterday Leena's birthday present from Adam and family in Berlin finally arrived. At 5.30pm a delivery man appeared with a large yellow cardboard box that weighed nothing. Leena couldn't understand what it might contain and wasted no time in opening it. And what did she find? Rolled-up cardboard and a crunched-up paper-bag from a well-known German supermarket chain, like the children's party game of pass-the-parcel. But then there was something at the bottom of the box, in a large sheet of bubble-wrap was a nicely wrapped rectangular parcel with three cards taped to the top, one from Allan and

Elida, one from Amelia where she had written quite nicely, and one with scribbles in many colours from Lea. It was a framed photo, not one, but a collage of the best and most colourful photos of the girls. Allan and Elida only featured in two of them. A gift done with much loving care and thought. She rang them right away to thank them. Amelia wanted to know which photo she liked best. It is now hanging in pride of place on the hallway wall where everybody entering the house can see it.

Today is a different kind of day – the five-year anniversary since Tom passed away. Sam and Leena met at the cemetery, Leena on foot and Sam having arrived by train from Charing Cross. Leena had planted the red begonias she bought at the garden centre a few days previously – red being Tom's favourite colour. Sam had already watered the flowers before she got there. They stayed for a while, sitting on a bench, saying not very much, regretting that Allan couldn't be there. If times had been normal, he might well have flown over for the occasion. After that they walked into the nature reserve close by where they sat down in the grass and had a picnic. People, who would normally have been at work, walking and cycling by. Sam had never been to the reserve, didn't even know it existed. Leena was there only a few days ago, but she still managed to get them lost on the way back. Instead of ending up by the main road, as intended, they finished up near the big Tesco, which was fine really. Sam said, "They say I'm hopeless with directions, but you are worse." And all the time the sun was shining.

June 1st, 2020

3 o'clock, be it early morning or mid-afternoon, is a lifeless hour when time is wondering what to do. If you wake up in the night, the silence of the street will tell you that it must be around 3. The last night-owl has made it home, and the unfortunates who start work before everyone else, are still in bed. 3pm has the same feel – the day hovering between noon and early afternoon. In her childhood home in Norway – the time when her mother would bake waffles or take home-made buns out of the freezer for afternoon coffee. A time Leena used to dislike because the day seemed to have ground to a halt. But now she is not so sure – the sun still high in the sky, its rays beating down on the earth. The leaves in the canopy above shivering in a subtle breeze. Nature at a standstill, like her life and she's getting used to it, perhaps even beginning to like it; days with nothing special to do, the life of a prisoner, which we all are, prisoners of a virus that refuses to go away. As Camus says in *the Outsider*: "On finit toujours par s'habituer à tout." – *In the end you get used to everything . . .*

This morning Allan rang her, well-meaning, wanting to see how she's getting on. It's a bank holiday in Germany, and a beautiful day to boot. The weather is nice in England as well, the air still, the sky nearly white as it has been several days running.

Allan's in-laws, German Arthur and Brazilian Antonia, arrived by car yesterday, from their home near Stuttgart, ostensibly to help look after the children so Allan and Elida can get on with their work. Their help is much needed, so all well and good. Leena knew about the plans for some

191

time. Naturally she would have loved to help out, but that's out of the question. The worst scenario is for her to catch the virus en route to Berlin and infect Allan and his family. Besides all means of travel between the two countries have been cut off. Later in the summer Allan and family will go on a road-trip ending in the in-law's home outside Stuttgart. It's good that they'll all be together, of course it is, and lovely for the girls to spend time with their doting grandparents. Much preferable to being in Berlin all summer. The original plan was for the family to spend two weeks in London with Leena, but that plan is off, naturally. So now they are going to Stuttgart instead.

All the same, while they are together, happy and laughing, Leena will be alone. When she finally gets to see her granddaughters again, they might not know what to say to each other.

Then again ... her father was cut off from his family, sailing on the world's oceans, carrying oil for the Allies, for close to seven years, before, during and after World War II. Leena has read the diaries he kept during the war, albeit irregularly, sitting in his captain's quarters, making the odd entry. He too had no idea how long it would take. In 1943 he wrote that he hoped to celebrate Christmas at home. Little did he know that it would take four more years before he'd see Berit and Hans again. When he finally caught up with them in Norway, neither of them was the same person who had said goodbye seven years before.

The world is not a stable place. You can't count on things not changing, or going well – that this year will be like last year, and next year will be much the same, that the anticipated holiday will go off without a hitch...Leena's family in Berlin may be out of reach, but one day, hopefully soon, it should be possible to take the Tube across London and go for a walk with Sam on the Walthamstow Marshes. She mentioned this to him, but he was not too keen. He was beginning to have had enough of local walks and suggested they meet up at Charing Cross instead for a walk in the royal parks.

*

For some time now, Leena has seen a tortoise shell cat running away when she comes out onto the decking. The cat looks glossy and well fed, so obviously not a stray, but she may still be on the look-out for a new home. However, she never comes inside or tries to make contact. For some genetic reason all tortoise shell cats are female, which is how Leena knows that it is a she.

Her days may look empty, but there is always something to do. The rose bushes and flower pots in the garden need watering. After that, another online choir practice is scheduled. Leena can't quite see the point as there isn't going to be a concert. Still, it makes a change and it helps keep the choir ticking over until better times. Besides, it is nice to see people again even if it's only on a screen. Regrettably, there is little time for conversation.

The tortoise shell cat is sleeping on the ogre's patio, stretched out, clearly enjoying the sunshine on the warm paving stones. The ogre has not been seen since returning from hospital. Leena only knows he is in there because of the nurses coming and going. Apart from that, the house looks totally lifeless. She is uncoiling the hose-pipe when she suddenly hears from next door, "Shoo! Go away! Shoo!" And there comes the poor cat bounding over the fence and disappears among the bushes on Leena's side. Out on his patio stands the ogre, dressed in a tatty brown dressing gown, spitting with rage and waving a broomstick. Definitely getting better. His brush with death clearly hasn't changed him at all. Soon he will start pestering Leena about the eucalyptus tree again.

After dinner, she watched *The Real Marigold Hotel* on BBC iPlayer. A series following a group of ageing celebrities, some would say has-beens, travelling to India to see if they fancied retiring there. The group included two larger-than-life personalities, the erstwhile sex-symbol Britt Ekland, perhaps better known for her colourful private life than her acting, bright and likeable. She wasted no opportunity to tell everyone she met that she had been a "Bond girl" in *The Man with a Golden Gun* back in 1974. The other dazzling character is the illustrious designer, Dame Zandra Rhodes, with her bright pink hair and enormous jewellery, known for her colourful fabric and dress designs. 76 and 78 years old, both wearing flamboyant clothes and both still sparkling. Retire? Whatever for? They love their lives, Ekland in California with her work, children and grandchildren, and Rhodes in London with her designs and interesting friends. They came for the ride, that was all – another adventure in an exciting life.

July 23rd, 2020

The harvest now is over,
The summer days are gone,
And yet no power cometh to help us.

These words are taken from the Old Testament in the story of the prophet, Elijah, who was born around 900 BC. They refer to a catastrophic drought during his lifetime that destroyed the Israelites' harvest.

Humankind has always had calamities to contend with. The earth was not created to provide a bed of roses for humans to lie on. Throughout history earthquakes, volcanic eruptions, tsunamis, droughts, floods, locusts and pestilence have hit and claimed lives when least expected.

The world has not changed. In olden and not so olden times people looked to the Lord for help. Some people probably still do, but Leena has never moved in their circles so there isn't much she can say about it.

As far as pestilence is concerned, people of later days have trusted their own ingenuity and science rather than invoking help from an invisible God.

*

Four months to the day since Britain went into lockdown. Strangely, Leena's journal entry for March 23rd does not mention lockdown at all. Instead, she writes at some length about her sojourns to Norway and Budapest, hankering back to a not-so-distant past when the world was open and you could go where you liked, when you liked.

Initially, lockdown didn't make a big difference to her life. Reading every day about the spread of the virus, she had chosen to keep a low profile anyway. A couple of times she'd bumped into friends she hadn't seen for a while. Oblivious to the virus, they'd given her a hug and a kiss on the cheek. She, however, had felt uncomfortable. She was happy to see them and didn't want to appear unfriendly, so she kept her reservations to herself, but the thought that they might know the virus was on her mind. A few days later, hugs and kisses would be out of the question for who knows how long.

At first lockdown was intended to last for three weeks, but a lot of people, including the powers that be, thought it might continue for much longer than that.

*

Pestilence is as old as humanity itself. The *Black Death*, which hit Europe in 1347, claimed an estimated 200 million lives in just four years. It originated in China from where it slowly made its way to Asia Minor and Europe. It was caused by flees on black rats carrying the Yersinia Pestis bacteria, and by 1346 it had spread to the Crimea, travelling along the Silk Road, killing an untold number of people along the way. From the Crimea, the plague was thought to have been transmitted by Oriental rat fleas that survived on the blood of black rats that regularly resided on merchant ships.

As for stopping the disease, people had no scientific understanding of contagion, but they knew that it had something to do with proximity. That's why forward-thinking officials in the Venetian-controlled port city of Ragusa decided to keep newly arrived sailors in isolation until they could prove they weren't sick. At first, sailors were held on their ships for 30 days, which became known in Venetian law as a *trentino*. As time went on, the Venetians increased the forced isolation to 40 days or a *quarantino*, the origin of the word quarantine and the start of its practice in the Western world.

The plague came to England in the late 1340s. A trading nation, the English still put out ships, with the understanding that they would comply with quarantines. The trouble was, people have to be alive to obey quarantine. In 1349, a ship carrying wool set out from England, bound for some destination in the north. During its journey, crew members started dying. Attempts to quarantine the sick on board failed. The plague took one person after another, until every last crew member died. The disease itself lived on in the other creatures aboard.

With some good luck, the ghost ship might have drifted on the sea until it sank, but the 14th century was not a century for good luck. The ship ran aground near Bergen harbour in Norway, where its living inhabitants – rats and fleas – made it into the country. Contemporary accounts, estimated that a third of the country's population died. Some estimates say closer to half. And so, it was that the plague reached far-away Norway in the creepiest way possible. From Norway, the plague spread to Sweden and by 1351 into Russia. So, a ghost ship unleashed an unimaginable horror on the country it drifted into. Sometimes horror movies get history right.

People at the time did not understand the spread of the disease. In Norway people imagined the shadowy figure of Pesta – the plague hag, who walked the countryside, flew over mountains or travelled by boat, thus reaching every nook and cranny of the country. She was the personification of the Black Death, ashen faced, dressed in a black cloak and a red skirt, carrying with her a rake and a broom, but sometimes only one or the other. If she approached a farm with only a rake, the people were relatively lucky, for some would escape by passing through the teeth of the rake. If she only carried a broom, they would all be swept away and perish.

July 24th, 2020

It is weird how your mind can play tricks on you and make you remember things totally differently from how they were. Looking back on the early days of lockdown, Leena could have sworn that the weather was overcast with a blustery wind and showers. Being a keen photographer and using your mobile instead of a camera, has its uses. All her photos are stored in her mobile with date and time of day:
March 22nd, 3:58pm, perfect blue sky. That was a Sunday and the trees in the little forest were without leaves.

March 23rd, 2:07pm, the day Britain went into lock-down. Photo of a Japanese cherry tree covered in the most unearthly white blossom, taken during a walk to the nature reserve – a trip she mentioned at the time, but forgot about later. The photos from that day, however, show brilliantly blue skies and geese and ducks on the lake in the reserve. Of course, thinking about it now, she remembers the papers showing pictures and writing about people congregating in vast numbers in parks and on beaches, ignoring the virus, despite having been told to stay indoors.

Keeping a journal can be a monotonous task when each day is more or less the same, so much so, that some days you don't bother to write anything at all. The point is that in her mind's eye these days were cloudy and chilly, when in fact they were sunny and warm. The horror of what was unfolding had crept into her bones and created memories in keeping with the situation.

And June … whatever happened to June? It just went. Only two clear memories spring to mind. June 4th, Amelia's birthday, which she was truly sad to miss. Amelia had accepted that she couldn't invite her friends, but she would still have a party with Mummy, Daddy and Lea, and Omma and Opa, her maternal grandparents, who had driven up from Stuttgart. Allan rang at 3 o'clock when Amelia was about to open her presents, beginning with the things Leena had sent her, which fortunately she loved. They kept up the FaceTime contact so Leena in her suburb and Sam in Walthamstow could take part in the celebration. Then there was the cake, baked by Elida and decorated by Amelia with unbelievable amounts of chocolates and smarties on top. They all sat around the table, leaving symbolic chairs for Leena and Sam. Allan asked if they had a piece of cake to make it seem even more real, which Leena had, but not Sam. So, she was sharing in the festivities, happy to be included, a joyous occasion. But thinking about it now, it brings tears to her eyes. Families aren't meant to be separated like that.

On June 19th, she went by train to Charing Cross where she met up with Sam for a walk in St James's Park and Green Park. From a near-empty station they passed through Trafalgar Square which was as good as deserted, not even a pigeon to be seen. No children climbing on the lions, in fact they were cordoned off. A handful of people, mostly men, were scattered on steps and benches around the perimeter, but that was all. The parks were glorious as always, but with very few people, it felt more like a stroll in the country than a walk in a London Park. The lack of people made them notice trees and plants they must have walked past many times without seeing. They sat down on a bench in St James's Park enjoying a lunch of sandwiches, crisps and strawberries Leena had prepared at home, knowing that the food outlets in London would be closed. The sky was mostly overcast, but every now and again the sun came peeping out, making it feel lovely and warm. In addition, there was the euphoria of having escaped from her suburb, all be it for only a few hours. The last time she'd set foot outside her local area was on the 15th of March, so it had been an extended form of house arrest, really.

So, there you are, one month of her life slipped by leaving next to no memory. Days with nowhere special to go and nothing to do that cannot be postponed until tomorrow, if not tomorrow, then perhaps the day after ... Leena knows she is not in a good place when she can't see the point in getting up in the morning. But up she gets, forces herself to shower and dress. Puts on her makeup, makes a point of going out, exchange a few words with someone, be it a passing neighbour, a supermarket assistant or a friendly person in the street. Time spent on e-mail and Facebook. People write to her, she writes back. She posts photos on Facebook, people click *like*. She clicks *like* on other people's photos and posts, makes the odd comment. A tenuous contact with the outside world. Allan and Sam call her every day. There is her friend, Gerda, in Norway, also a keen photographer. They write and send each other photos on Messenger. Then, there is her lockdown journal, which she tries to keep up. The house needs to be kept clean ...

Leena knows a woman, Cora, who has lost all motivation and shuffles about in her nightgown all day, spending hours watching day-time TV. Apart from being 72 and having a mild form of Type 2 diabetes, she was fine before lockdown. But then she heeded Mr Johnson's directive, accepted that she's old and vulnerable and barricaded herself indoors, didn't even sneak out for a solitary walk around the block. And of course, no visitors. Leena shudders to think what her home must look like.

How you cope with a situation like lockdown very much depends on your personal disposition. Leena has always been self-sufficient. Her mother put it like this once when they were talking, "You and Hans were forever busy doing something when you were children, but John often complained about being bored." Thinking about Cora, she seemed always to be running off to classes and clubs and lunches and what have you – things that involve socialising, and here she is, totally destroyed.

Whatever your personal makeup and whichever way you try to cope, the fact remains, human beings simply are not made for the emptiness of isolation. There is a reason why solitary confinement is considered worse than an ordinary prison sentence. This, when all is said and done, is the tragedy of a pandemic – the necessity to isolate in order to protect yourself and others from the virus. People born at the beginning of the 20th century had all sorts of disasters to contend with – World War 1, Spanish flu, the worldwide recession of the 1930s, World War 2 … People in the Western world, born after 1945, have never lived through a calamity. Consequently, we are ill-equipped to weather a long-lasting pandemic.

*

The sky is a luminous white. Again, a fine blanket of ice crystals is spread out between heaven and earth, with a few wispy clouds floating lower down. She used like the white sky – associating it with the beginning of a glorious summer's day, which must have been when she first noticed the phenomenon. But now it looks vacant, empty like her life. Leena doesn't much like July either – a month when time seems to stand still. The vibrant colours of spring and early summer are gone. The days are getting shorter. The colours are more muted. Nature is stagnant, silently preparing for things to change.

As a child in Norway, she loved August, with its first cool breath of autumn in the air. Back at school, seeing her classmates for the first time in two months. Swallows gathering on power lines above yellow barley fields, preparing for their long journey to Egypt, their tiny brains telling them exactly where to go. Crickets in the grass striking up the first notes for the evening's concert. Still warm. Leena walking home during the first week of school. A few days of excitement before the dreariness of old Mr Johansen's teaching took over.

*

When your life seems hopeless, you look back at better days, searching for remnants of the good days concealed in the present. The fields must have turned yellow by now, but without a car it is difficult for Leena to get out into the country to see them, without spending ages on buses which she doesn't really want to do. Yesterday she saw a small flock of starlings zooming about the sky. The rowan berries are red and ripe, as they will soon be in her beloved Norway. Sam will come for late lunch-early dinner. Leena will cook paella without the chicken as she has done so many times before. Yes, much of the past is still around, you just need to close your eyes and bring it into focus.

It is interesting to note how officials with slow communication and limited medical knowledge took more decisive action to stop the great plague of London back in the 1660s than the Johnson administration could muster in 2020.

When reports of plague around Europe began to reach England in the 1660s, it caused the Privy Council to take steps to prevent it crossing to England. Quarantining of ships had been used during previous outbreaks and was introduced for ships coming to London in November 1663, following outbreaks in Amsterdam and Hamburg. Two naval ships were assigned to intercept any vessels entering the Thames estuary. Ships from infected ports were required to moor at Hole Haven on Canvey Island for a period of 30 days before being allowed to travel up-river. Ships from ports free of plague or completing their isolation period were given a certificate of health and allowed to travel on. A second inspection line was established between the forts on opposite banks of the Thames at Tilbury and Gravesend with instructions only to pass ships with a certificate. The isolation period was increased to forty days in May 1664 as the continental plague worsened. Regulations were enforced quite strictly, so that people or houses where voyagers had come ashore without serving their quarantine were also subjected to 40 days of isolation.

The earliest cases of disease occurred in the spring of 1665 in a parish outside the city walls called St

Giles-in-the-Fields. The death rate began to rise during the hot summer months and peaked in September when 7,165 Londoners died in one week.

The rats that carried the fleas that caused the plague were attracted by city streets filled with rubbish and waste, especially in the poorest areas.

Those who could, including most doctors, lawyers and merchants, fled the city. Charles II and his courtiers left in July for Hampton Court and then Oxford. Parliament was postponed and had to sit in October at Oxford, the spread of the plague being so dreadful. Court cases were also moved from Westminster to Oxford.

The Lord Mayor and aldermen remained to enforce the King's orders to try and stop the spread of the disease. The poorest people remained in London with the rats and people with the plague. Watchmen locked and kept guard over infected houses. Parish officials provided food. Searchers looked for dead bodies, loaded them on carts and took them at night to plague pits for burial.

All trade with London and other plague towns was stopped. The Council of Scotland declared that the border with England would be closed. There were to be no fairs or trade with other countries. This meant many people lost their jobs – from servants to shoemakers and those who worked on the River Thames.

As if one calamity was not enough ... The Great Fire of London raged from 2-6 September 1666 and gutted the Medieval City of London inside the Roman city walls where the poorest sections of the population lived. The fire did, however, quell the worst of the plague as it killed the rats that were spreading it.

*

Only recently are Johnson & Co hinting that perhaps mistakes were made during the early days of the pandemic, and that perhaps lockdown should have been introduced sooner. Nevertheless, they maintain that they were following scientific advice every step of the way. Their explanation, or rather excuse, is that they didn't understand the virus. However, they must have been aware of the full outbreaks unfolding in Italy and Spain. The countries that dealt with the pandemic efficiently did not quite understand the virus either. Still, their presidents or prime ministers, incidentally many of them women, did understand that this looked serious, and it is better to take decisive preventive measures sooner rather than later.

So, how does a pandemic end? Apparently, there are two different endings and neither is clearly defined. There is the end caused when there are no more cases of the disease, which can take time as there can be several spikes and recurrences before no more cases are noted. This could be due to herd immunity or because the virus has weakened and become less deadly. A strain of the Spanish flu virus is still surviving as ordinary flu. Or, it could end when an effective vaccine has been invented and made widely available, as happened with polio. The virus is still around but few cases are noted due to the vaccine. The other type of ending is when people decide that they have had enough of all the restrictions and decide to try to get on with their lives even if the disease is still around. This ending has more to do with economic considerations than concerns for people's health. This seems to be where we are at the moment: people are fed up and the economy needs to recover before suffering further devastation.

Still July 24th, Breaking News

Chaos reigns in shops, train stations and cafés as face masks become compulsory today.

Brawls break out in supermarkets with customers wearing masks attacking people who don't.

McDonald's kicks out diners not covering up.

Asda, Sainsbury and Co-op refuse to enforce rules today.

The new rules cover shops, stations, banks, post offices, shopping centres and petrol stations.

Failure to comply could result in a £100 fine, but the police indicate they will only respond as a last resort.

Only young children and people with medical conditions are exempt from the new rules.

McDonald's said takeaway customers will be forced to wear a mask, but people eating in the restaurant will not.

Very sensible too. Leena was wondering how people could be expected to eat wearing a face mask.

July 26th, 2020, Breaking News

Chaos as air bridge to Costas is axed overnight! Brits in Spain are ordered into 14-day quarantine on their return and trips for thousands are hit as essential-only travel advice kicks in after new Covid outbreak – amid warnings of more countries to follow.

Tourists who had jetted off to the Mediterranean when Boris Johnson's ministers insisted it was safe were furious after learning that the air bridge scheme, which should let them back without restrictions, was effectively withdrawn.

This sowed uncertainty across the travel industry last night, combined with fears other countries could soon fall off the safe travel list.

All the same … People must have known that Covid-19 is a pandemic in flux, that things can change very quickly. When the travel restrictions to Spain were lifted, things looked good, but now, with renewed incidents in Spain and some other countries, things look less good, hence the reintroduction of restrictions. Alas, today's people don't seem to have the fortitude or stamina and social concern to sit out a calamity for as long as it takes. Holidaymakers returning from Spain are whinging about the prospect of 14 days' quarantine, like a spoilt child screaming, "But you promised me an ice-cream!" The same can be said for those who flock to restaurants and beaches because it is allowed and forget all about social distancing. Never mind that the virus is still out there and that they stand a chance of being infected, and in turn infecting others. The virus can only live in the body for 14 days. If by then it has not found a new body to enter, it will perish. Information about the ways of Covid-19 has been part of daily life for so long that it is baffling how so many people have failed to grasp it. Instead they keep whining: "We've been living under lockdown for too long, it's time we had some fun!"

*

So that's it then, so far. The raw figures are grim. Britain has the worst overall Covid-19 death toll in Europe, with more than 46,000 dead according to official figures, whilst also suffering the continent's second-worst "excess death" tally per capita, more than double France's and eight times higher than Germany's. It did not protect its oldest and most vulnerable, who died in nursing homes in appalling numbers. It allowed the disease to spread throughout the country rather than isolating it in one area. It failed to close its borders in good time, abandoned contact tracing too early, set targets that were missed, designed government programmes that didn't work, and somehow contrived to let the three most senior figures overseeing its pandemic response, including the prime minister, catch the very virus they were fighting. Now it faces the worst recession of any developed country, according to the Organization for Economic Cooperation and Development, and is once again taking a gamble by easing its lockdown at a relatively early stage.

July 27th, 2020

Enough, nok, genug, bastante, ça suffit, suficiente, halas.

Leena is tidying the kitchen, loading the dishwasher, wiping the surfaces with disinfectant.

After that, retrieving her large suitcase from the loft. Having got travelling with hand luggage-only down to a fine art, she hasn't used this case for some time, but now it will be filled to bursting.

In go underwear, nightwear, two thick jumpers, quilted jacket and body warmer, both of them red. Smart trousers, jeans, her Ugg boots, toiletries, blouses, T-shirts…that's it, no more room. Her laptop will go in her handbag – it's all fine. There are shops where she's going as well. As an afterthought she wraps a cobalt blue glass bird in a nightgown and places it among her clothes.

Time is not in plentiful supply. She needs to be at Herne Hill station at 3pm to allow for things going wrong on the way to Luton Airport.

Herne Hill, the insignificant station on one of the many railway lines terminating at London Victoria. Passed unnoticed for years until it acquired the rose-tinted glow of nostalgia as the gateway to Budapest. How many times did she visit Sam during the two years that he lived there, four or five? She can't remember exactly. Whatever the season, Budapest was always glorious – the little cafés, Freedom Bridge, the Danube, Margit Island, the wonderful old buildings, Sam's and Aurora's flat in a late 19th century block, built around an old-world inner courtyard … But then Sam and Aurora split up and Sam returned to London. In hindsight she remembers waiting for Thames Link at Herne Hill as always happening in the morning, but it couldn't have been. A couple of times, definitely, but she also remembers arriving in Budapest after dark, so even with Budapest being one hour ahead, she must have left later in the day, at least once or twice.

Her train arrives. Leena quickly fastens her face mask, which she had loosened whilst waiting, and lugs her heavy case onto the train. Plenty of empty seats. The familiar stations; Elephant & Castle, Black Friars, Farringdon, St Albans and Luton.

The sky is grey and overcast, a few raindrops hitting the windows. Crossing the Thames, stopping at Farringdon where Allan once worked and they all used to meet up for a pizza – Tom was alive then, and Amelia was yet to be born. Passing Alexandra Palace in the distance, like a fairy-tale castle, then through open countryside, fields yellow and ripe, some of which have already been harvested. She is even using the same airline as back then – Wizz air. She thought they only flew to Eastern Europe, but it turns out they provide budget flights all over the place.

It wasn't reports about Covid-19 being on the rise, not only in Spain but in many other countries as well, that prompted Leena to pack her bags and leave. The decision was made more than a week ago, although she was not aware of it at the time. It was a hot day, with the cloying humid air that Leena has always hated because it saps her energy and makes her feel heavy and sluggish. She had been shopping at M&S and was sitting on a bench at the bus stop. A pleasant spot with two wooden benches opposite an old church. The bus wasn't due for another five minutes. That was when she became aware of a middle-aged man sitting on the other bench, plenty of distance between them, so no problem there, but he kept blowing his nose, loudly and thoroughly, again and again, into a large old-fashioned handkerchief. There's dirt and there's dirt. Leena's mother used to talk about clean dirt, the kind you find on a kid who has been making mud pies, or a workman after labouring all day on a building site or digging a ditch, men who will take off their muddy clothing and have a shower the minute they get home. Then there is the kind of slowly accumulated grime when a person hasn't had a proper wash or change of clothes in weeks – the sort that makes you want to lift an individual by the scruff of the neck, preferably with a boat hook, dip the entire person, clothes and all, into a basin of disinfectant and watch the dirt floating away. The man on the bench belonged to the second category. The bus arrived, and Leena was disconcerted to find him entering close behind her, he wasn't wearing a mask, and sat down diagonally opposite her, coughing. These days there is a notice on the entrance door saying, "Maximum 11 passengers allowed", and of course face masks are obligatory. Apart from the man and Leena there are five more individuals on the bus. A woman in her early 30s, her face mask loosened and dangling around her neck, is talking happily into her phone. A young man is wearing a mask, but it's only covering his mouth and not his nose. The woman finishes her conversation but doesn't pull up her mask. The other passengers – three elderly women – are all wearing masks. One of them, however, is only covering her mouth. Out of seven passengers only three are covering mouth and nose like they're supposed to. Haven't those people understood anything? That they are supposed to cover their mouth and nose for a reason! Don't they know how the respiratory system works? With people like that there really is no hope. It's only a short bus-ride, six stops in all. The grimy man leaves two stops before Leena, making sure to touch every handle bar with his infested hands on his way out. Oh, the feelings of disgust – virus covering every surface, virus permeating the hot cloying air, making you want to stop breathing. She has witnessed similar scenes many times before – people happily spreading their filth. Leena manages to get out without touching anything, which, carrying two shopping bags, is quite a feat. Don't tell her that public transport is safe!

Finally, outside, drawing a deep breath, she tears off her face-mask, folds it up and stuffs it in a pocket in her handbag. The street looks happy and normal – tall trees, the flowers of late summer, mainly dahlias, the neat houses and gardens of a respectable London suburb. She retreats to her home like a frightened animal to its burrow. No curtains, only blinds to be drawn at night, her windowsills filled with colourful glass, mostly from the ancient glass factory in Norway. One window has only blue glass, one has red, and one has green. She and Nina would drive there every year, buying one or two pieces, always red, green or blue, but these days Nina can't be bothered. There are other objects as well, treasures her father brought from around the world salvaged from the house in the forest, a painting of a Norwegian mountain landscape, a beautiful Chinese rug . . .

*

There used to be a long queue and a scramble to get on the bus taking passengers the short distance from the station to the airport, but not so this time. There were only a few passengers, all of them wearing face masks.

Last time she came here, the lounges were teaming with people. Now there were very few. The Reykjavik plane was up on the board; departure 19:10, but no gate number as yet. Leena felt such a sense of relief. Iceland – one of the few countries in the world where Covid-19 has been eradicated. A country she has never seen, whose language she can read up to a point, but not speak. In the late 8th century AD, when Norwegian settlers began to colonise Iceland, they brought with them their language, Old Norse, the language of the Vikings. Over the centuries, the languages of mainland Scandinavia changed beyond recognition. Norwegian, Swedish and Danish developed along similar lines and are basically variations of the same language. In Iceland, the language remained largely unchanged – like the difference between modern Italian and Latin. Thus, a Norwegian can understand written Icelandic well enough to half-follow a text, but that's all. Come to think about it … wouldn't it be tantalising if an island existed somewhere, where people still speak Latin?

Clean air, clean landscape, clean sea. No crowds spreading a deadly virus. Northern lights in winter, proper ones, not just an echo like you find in southern Norway. And her sons … They'll come, especially Sam, he is looking forward to it already. As for Allan and his family … they can't see each other anyway, so what difference does it make whether she lives in England or Iceland? At least now she has a better chance of surviving Covid, to see the day when she can reclaim her place within her family – to see Amelia and Lea grow up.

She'll spend a few nights with a friend from her working days. After that she'll rent a small house somewhere, with a view of a bay where she can see whales. Early morning walks, filling her lungs with air so cool and pure you can drink it, watching whales frolic in the cold clean waters of the bay.

The airport was very quiet. Everybody needed to wear a mask at the airport and also on the plane. It is more difficult talking to people when checking in baggage as you can't hear or understand one another, like moving among ghosts, and she found the security part rather stressful, as always. She could have done with a drink, but how can you have a drink with a face mask? A friend had advised her to pre-book a Covid test at Reykjavik airport, which she had done, and been promised that trained nurses would be waiting for them at passport security and that they would be taken to separate cubicles for their test. What she would then have to do, was to isolate for 24 hours until she had the result which, all being well, would be negative. Her friend had a room for her to isolate in, so that shouldn't be a problem.

And all the while a deep sense of unreality. She knows what she is fleeing from, but not exactly what she is fleeing to. Like the dream she had last night. She was going on holiday to Israel, and was nearly at the airport when it suddenly hit her: she had left her travel documents and camera at home. It was too late to go back and collect them. Thinking quickly, she realised that she didn't really need the documents, but going on a special holiday without being able to take pictures was unthinkable. Panic and chaos ensued, something about her debit card inexplicably having been cut to pieces and the plane being delayed and all the passengers being given a brown paper bag with food and a glass of juice ... A dream soon fragmented by the clear light of day.

Finally, on the plane. Leena kept waiting for the rest of the passengers to arrive, until it dawned on her that there was no rest of the passengers, the flight only had about 25-30 people on it, so most of them, Leena included, got a row of seats to themselves.

August 4th, 2020, Eyjafjörður

The landscape of Northern Iceland is wild and rugged, covered in grass, moss and lichen. No trees. The sea is often choppy with brown seaweed sloshing about in the surf. Not many ships passing. The air is cool and crisp, and this morning the sky is blue and without cloud after a spell of grey foggy weather. The house, temporarily serving as Leena's home, looks like a square box from the distance, red, covered in painted corrugated iron, like so many houses in Iceland. Inside, however, it's pleasant – photos and paintings by local artists on the walls. Chairs that have seen some use, especially by a large hairy dog. Crocheted off-white curtains, rag-rugs on the wooden floors, also showing evidence of a dog.

A rented silver Honda is parked outside, Leena's for the duration of her stay. This is not London with buses and Tubes and what-have-you every few minutes. Either you drive to the shops, or you cycle or walk for miles. She totally refuses to drive in the London traffic, but here it's a different story. Just one road, going to Akureyri, Iceland's second largest city, or rather town. Roads branching off to other small towns, and to Vatnajökull, Iceland's largest glacier. Leena hasn't been there yet, but she'll drive down one day soon. The house is so quiet. All you hear is the wind and sometimes birds flying and cackling overhead. Leena has a strong reclusive streak, she loves the serenity and mindfulness of being alone, doing nothing, just listening to the silence. It was what she had hoped for on her visits to her childhood home in Norway, but family members got in the way. These days the ethos is constantly to be doing something, to be on the go, running from one appointment to the next. How often have you heard the phrase, "People with today's busy lifestyles", suggesting that always being on the go is what we should strive for. The English language has idioms for doing nothing, all of them with negative connotations – twiddling your thumbs, smelling the roses, watching the grass grow ... but why not? Being a solitary person, Leena was basically fine with lockdown even though it could get a bit much at times. For families cooped up in small inner city flats it was of course a different story, as it was for people forever craving company and action.

6am. The dog, Mirra, a gigantic brown Leonberger, is standing by the door, whining. She is old and cranky but

217

she can't get out of her life-long habit of going for a wee first thing in the morning, whether she needs to or not. "All right, all right, patience, I'm coming!" Leena throws on an anorak, sticks her feet in an old pair of trainers that she found in a closet, and off they go. Leena likes dogs, and Mirra has taken to her already.

So, how did Leena end up here, in charge of a dog? Long story. A friend of a friend needed somebody to house-sit and dog-sit for a couple of months while he was away at sea, he was the chief engineer of a large fishing vessel, and his wife had recently passed away. No rent, just look after the dog, and make the house look inhabited, in case an uninvited guest should be on the prowl; it happens, even here.

The morning was crisp and calm as they sauntered down the field to the shore, the late-summer sun had already cleared the top of the mountain. Mirra was loving its relative warmth despite clearly being quite frail. Half way to the shore, she sat down in the middle of the path and started one of her marathon scratching sessions and Leena just stood by and waited. That was when they heard the whale blow – like the sound horses make when they blow or snort, similar to that, but magnified ten times. It is as though you can hear their enormous size in the sound. They both turned on the spot, just in time to see the gorgeous glistening black whale rolling in the sun-sparkling surface of the fjord, directly off shore from where they were standing. How close? Hard to tell as the bank is five metres or so down to the shore and they were about 25 metres from the edge of the bank. Direct line of sight just caught the whale, so probably around 50–70 metres, 100 metres max. This was what Leena had hoped for, almost come for. She had been told whales come in to Eyjafjörður, but she had never fully believed she'd be lucky enough to see one. How long did they stand there? Leena has no idea. It could have been one minute it could have been ten. She'll forever cherish that moment with Mirra, watching the whale disappearing into the calm shimmering depths. Virginia Wolf talked about moments of being; this was most certainly one such moment, unforgettable and entirely magical.

END

Other Books by
this Author

Flight of the Albatross

ISBN: 978-1-910757-23-9

My father never talked about his life as the captain of an oil tanker during World War 2. I was born after the War and his life at sea continued throughout my childhood and into my teens. The places he visited, the letters that arrived with colourful stamps from countries nobody had heard of and the objects he brought back from distant lands fired my imagination and made me want to emulate his life.

I knew very little about my father's life in the convoys. It was only after I started researching this period that I got some idea of what it must have been like. And, importantly how the Norwegian sailors received little or no recognition for their bravery and contribution without which the Allied could not have won the War.

A Devil's Work

ISBN: 978-1-910757-68-0

The short stories in A Devil's Work takes us on a journey to the between world of outsiders.

We meet the oddball Mrs Blomm, a newcomer to a close-knit local community in the Norwegian country-side with a penchant for walking about naked; the lone traveller moving through countries on the Trans-Siberian railway, interpreting but not understanding what she sees; the successful mother and career woman who feels alien-ated and struggles to keep her persona from slipping; and sometimes outsiders—lone wolves—do terrible things.

Margrethe Alexandroni, author of Flight of the Albatross, has also published short stories and articles in English and Norwegian. She is a former Teaching Fellow: Department of Scandinavian Studies in the school of European Languages, Culture & Society, University College London.

The Little
Foundling

ISBN: 978-1-910757-04-8

The full moon had climbed higher in the sky, shining on the frost-covered ground. The wolf was sitting at the edge of the forest, its eyes resting on her where she stood at the window. The air was alive with the sounds of the forest and something that sounded like a baby crying. The murmur of the trees grew stronger, but the wolf was quiet, only the hum of the wind and the baby crying. A baby crying! How could that be? The sound of footsteps–she was coping less well with her solitude than she'd believed. Hearing things...But it was there, the distinctive sound of a baby crying.

Having lived most of her life in London, Leena returns to the house in the Norwegian forest where she grew up to live a simple life away from the clamour of the 21st century. It doesn't work. The wider world that called her away as a young woman still calls out to her some 40 years later. She answers the call and embarks on journeys to some of the most remote corners of the globe.

Margrethe Alexandroni, author of Flight of the Albatross and A Devil's Work and other Stories has also published articles and short stories in English and Norwegian. She is a former Teaching Fellow at the Department of Scandinavian Studies in the School of European languages, Cultures & Society, University College London.

Hans

ISBN: 978-1-9996931-9-0

Hans and Leena, brother and sister, born ten years apart, grow up in the countryside of Eastern Norway. Both fiercely ambitious and both wanting more from life than their birth place can offer. Hans wants to be an airline pilot and Leena wants to become a world-class pianist. They both work hard to achieve their goals; which, however, meet with little encouragement from their parents and extended family.A shotgun wedding at the age of 19 puts paid to Hans' ambition. One day he disappears without trace. Their parents move heaven and earth to find him, but to no avail. A detective, employed to track him down, returns empty-handed, saying that you cannot find someone who does not want to be found, and that very likely he is out there, somewhere. Their parents take comfort in this and live out their lives hoping that one day Hans will return.Meanwhile we follow Leena from Norway to France, Italy, London, the Cayman Islands and Cuba. She appears to be a successful professional woman, although we learn little about her exact career path. Eventually we discover the truth about Hans' disappearance and catch glimpses of him over the years, forever a fugitive. The questions remain; did Hans and Leena achieve their goals albeit in a roundabout way, and will they ever see each other again?